The Kite Making Handbook

David & Charles

Compiled by Rossella Guerra - Giuseppe Ferlenga
(gnomonica@libero.it)

Editing and layout Linda Perina

Graphics Arc-en-ciel

Drawings Michele Gambin

Photographs Luigi Ferrari - Verona, Club aquilonisti Lupi Volanti,
San Martino di Lupari - Padua

The following helped with this book Club aquilonisti Lupi
Volanti, San Martino di Lupari - Padua, Alberto Merlo, Margherita
Sciaretta, Marco Zanoni

Coordination Renzo Zanoni

The editor is available to settle copyright issues for any photographs
for which it was impossible to find a source.

A DAVID & CHARLES BOOK

First published in the UK in 2004
Originally published as *Il grande libro degli aquiloni*
by Giunti Gruppo Editoriale, Florence, under licence
from Demetra S.r.l., Italy 2002

Distributed in North America
by F&W Publications, Inc.
4700 East Galbraith Road
Cincinnati, OH 45236
1-800-289-0963

A catalogue record for this book is available from the British Library.

ISBN 0 7153 1855 1 paperback

Printed in Singapore by KHL Printing Co Ltd
for David & Charles
Brunel House   Newton Abbot   Devon

Visit our website at www.davidandcharles.co.uk

David & Charles books are available from all good bookshops; alter-
natively you can contact our Orderline on (0)1626 334555 or write to
us at FREEPOST EX2110, David & Charles Direct, Newton Abbot,
TQ12 4ZZ (no stamp required UK mainland).

Some people think that kites are just toys for children, while others believe that they are extremely important for various aspects of science and technology. Both kinds of people hope that kites will continue to be the source of enjoyment and fascination that they have always been.

Where did kites originate? What do they symbolize? What kind of scientific experiments have they been used for? Can they be used for dragging boats or for carrying observation and photographic equipment – or even radio aerials – to high altitudes?

How many different kinds of kites are there? How can you learn to build them? What kind of materials and equipment do you need? Where can you find tips about flying them?

A multi-coloured rainbow made of kites connected to each other by their wing traverses.

Do kites date from prehistoric times?

Kites were already known in the Orient before history was written down. Like the Australian boomerang, they could date back to prehistoric times.

Maybe the first kite was inspired by the flight of a bird, the hat of a peasant or the sail of a ship swelling with the movement of the wind.

Kites have many different meanings in the Orient – religious, mystical or even theatrical. They are used for celebrating happy occasions such as a birth or victory.

On the fifth day of the fifth month in Japan, huge kites in the form of carps are flown to celebrate the birth of sons. Each carp swims upstream and represents a boy who will overcome many obstacles as he grows to manhood.

In Korea, it was a tradition to write the name and date of birth of a boy child on a kite before launching it. When the kite reached a certain height, the flying line was cut, so that the wind would carry the kite as far away as possible. It was believed that evil spirits would follow the kite, so that the boy would be left free of their influence.

In old Siam (now Thailand), people liked to fight with kites. There were two teams – first the Papkaos, which represented femininity and used light, manoeuvrable kites with tails. The other team, the Chulas, represented masculinity and used heavier, slower kites without tails. The Papkaos would try to capture the other team's kites by means of a lasso. The kites of the Chulas were equipped with sharp pieces of glass – the object was to cut the towlines of the other team's kites.

Again in Siam, people asked kites to capture the winds and attract them away, taking heavy rain clouds with them.

According to a Malaysian legend, kites would come to life as soon as they took to the sky.

In Polynesia, kites represented the point where the gods and mortals met. Rehua, who was the god of both health and the sky, was also the ancestor of all kites.

On the ninth day of the ninth month in China, kites were flown to foretell how successful their owners would be in their work. The higher the kite flew, the more successful its owner would become.

In about 200BC, a Chinese general called Han Hsin was laying siege to an opposing fortress. He flew a kite above its walls so that he could measure the distance between the fortress and his army. From this, he was able to calculate exactly the length of the tunnel which had to be dug to get into the fortress.

Kites were used by the Emperor Liang Mao (500AD) to recall his army after he had sent many of his soldiers home because they missed working in their fields. He ordered them to present themselves at his palace when they saw the kites flying. The enemy struck suddenly and laid siege to the palace. The Emperor ordered his general to launch the kites, and the army gathered a short distance from the palace. The enemy had not been able to understand the message sent by the kites, and they were soon defeated.

When were kites discovered in the West?

In the West, kites have been discovered and forgotten several times. One story attributes the introduction of kites into the Western world to Architas of Taranto (460–430BC). He was a Greek general, philosopher and politician, who is thought to have been inspired by Chinese birds to make a wooden dove, which he managed to make fly.

The Roman courts used to be preceded by a *draconarius*. This was a rod with a dragon's head on the top. The body was made of a tube of fabric that swelled in the wind.

A Neapolitan scientist and man of letters, Giambattista della Porta (1535–1615), wrote a treatise on the secrets of nature in 1589 (*Della Magia Naturale – On Natural Magic*). In this treatise, he described illuminated and musical kites, which were used for setting off fireworks.

In Sicily, kites were launched after sunset and let go until they disappeared from sight – according to tradition, when they returned to the ground they left a star in the sky in their place.

- **England**   *kite*
  The name of a bird of prey.

- **Italy**   *aquilone*
  The name of the cold north wind, or kite.

- **Germany**   *Drachen*
  The word for dragon, or kite.

- **Spain**   *cometa*
  The word for comet, or kite.

- **France**   *cerf-volant*
  Flying deer, or kite.

- **Brazil**   *papagayo*
  The word for parrot, or kite.

- **Japan**   *tako*
  The word for octopus, or kite.

- **China**   *feng cheng*
  The term for Aeolian harp, or kite.

A train of stunt kites at a kite festival.

Kites used in scientific experiments

From 1700, kites were used to compile information about weather conditions. Benjamin Franklin (1706–90), the American writer, scientist and politician, used them in an experiment he carried out to study electricity in the atmosphere.

Guglielmo Marconi (1874–1937), the Italian scientist who invented wireless telegraphy, launched a kite with an aerial to a height of 122m (400ft) to help establish a radio link between Greenland and the island of Newfoundland.

B.F.S. Baden-Powell, a well-known English balloonist and brother of Lord Robert Baden-Powell, the founder of the Boy Scouts Organisation, lifted a man with a single kite at Pirbright Camp, England, on 27 January 1894. The idea behind this was to provide the army with a means of aerial observation.

Even before this, an American schoolteacher called George Pocock had managed to lift his daughter Martha 90m (300ft) into the air, using an armchair attached to a kite.

Pocock also travelled 200km (125 miles) through the English countryside in a lightweight carriage towed by a kite.

Nowadays, kites are used for scientific research, in particular for studying the atmosphere and the weather. They are also used in radio broadcasting and for taking aerial photographs. The army has made use of kites for signalling and observation missions.

Kites have also been used for launching and displaying advertising banners.

Materials and Equipment

Birds riding the wind

Kites are anchored to the ground by means of a line. Only the power of the wind keeps them up in the air.

Kites are aerodynes which use the action of the wind to keep aloft. They are made up of a carrying structure or frame, a bridle and sails.

Wingspan Just like in aeroplanes, this is the width of a kite measured from wing tip to wing tip.

Frame The ribbing or skeleton of the kite. It is an assembly of rigid elements which make up the framework of the kite, over which the sails or covering are stretched.

The frame is made up of longerons, or spines, and traverses, or spars.

The frame should keep the sails or covering taut, and it must be light and strong.

Sails or covering The lightweight fabric or paper that covers the kite frame. It is activated by the power of the wind to lift the kite and make it fly.

Wind brace This is a line which follows the edge of the kite. It is attached to the ribbing, or frame, in order to strengthen it and make sure that it remains in the correct shape.

Bridle This is made up of at least two lines. It distributes tractive force on the kite and maintains it in the correct arrangement when it is flying.

Joints These are linking devices which, together with the fastenings, join the various parts of the kite to each other.

Ventral fin This is a vertical component made of fabric or paper. It performs a stabilizing function.

Towline Used for towing the kite. It makes sure that the kite is attached to its handler.

Winding reel Used for winding the towline in and out.

Tail This is essential for providing stability in some kites – particularly flat or plane surface kites.

Aeroplanes are derived from kites. As far back as 1900, the Wright Brothers managed to launch a large biplane. They steered it from the ground by means of two strong cables.

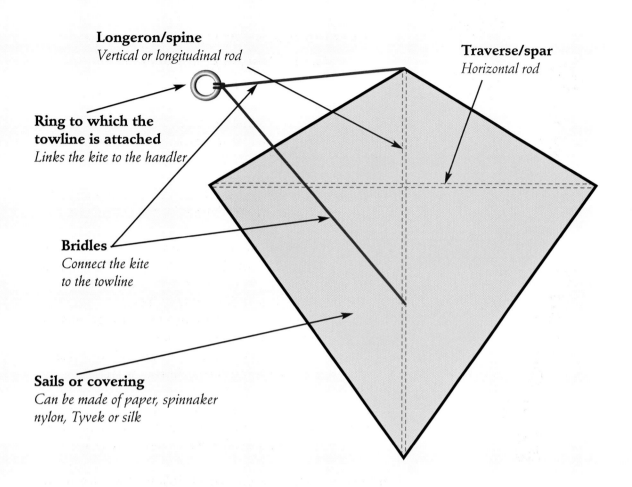

Longeron/spine
Vertical or longitudinal rod

Traverse/spar
Horizontal rod

Ring to which the towline is attached
Links the kite to the handler

Bridles
Connect the kite to the towline

Sails or covering
Can be made of paper, spinnaker nylon, Tyvek or silk

Ventral fin or keel
In many kites, the bridle is replaced by the keel, which is a triangular piece of material

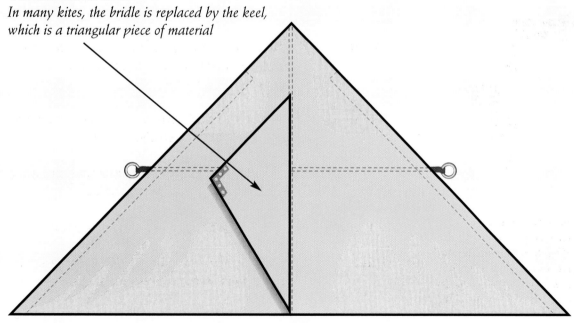

Kites and more kites

Kites are divided into categories according to their aerodynamic characteristics. There are plane surface or flat kites, bowed kites, cellular or box kites, and flexible or limp-wing kites.

Plane surface or flat kites

These are the simplest kinds of kites. They have a plane, or flat, surface.

They are suitable for stable, medium winds, and are very reliable due to their sail/weight ratio.

A plane surface kite needs a tail to keep it stable.

Lozenge or Diamond Kite

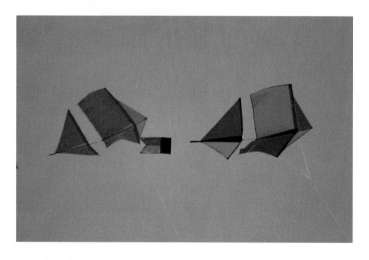

Kites based on the Japanese Sanjo Rokkaku kite

Bowed kites

The surface of the kite is curved, providing a wingspan with a positive dihedral angle, which gives more stability. In fact, the flow of air that strikes the kite is split in two so that it exits from the wings symmetrically.

A long time ago on a remote farm in China, birds were devouring the crops.

So the peasants built kites in the shape of birds, and attached bangers and firecrackers to their tails.

The kites lifted the fireworks, which had long fuses and exploded in the air. The birds were terrified, not only by the noise but by the strange shape of the kites, and they flew away for good.

Nowadays people often stop to look up at the sky in wonder. In the old days, however, people looked to the sky for signs that indicated a hidden power or force.

Cellular or Box kites

These kites are made up of cells. The first one was invented by an Australian called Hargrave in 1893. Nowadays, wonderful three-dimensional Box kites are designed by young kite enthusiasts. They are made of spinnaker nylon and fibreglass or carbon-fibre rods. These kites have exceptional aerodynamic characteristics and can maintain stable flight in strong winds. They are not suitable for flying in light winds, due to their heavy weight in relation to their reduced sail surface.

Some of these kites can fly in a variety of wind conditions. One kind is the Delta Box kite, which has two triangular wings.

Lawrence Hargrave was born in Greenwich, London, in 1850. He emigrated to Australia, where he studied engineering and specialized in extensive research into aerodynamics. He was looking for a structure which would be capable of safe, stable flight.

In 1893 he designed a kite which had two supporting surfaces and two vertical stabilizing laterals. He separated the two functions by means of horizontal and vertical plane surfaces.

Because the box kite had such good lifting and safety characteristics, it was soon adopted in the whole of Europe as a means of carrying out meteorological observations. Kite trains that reached an altitude of more than 10,000m (6 miles) were constructed.

The towlines were made of metal, however, and were highly dangerous. They could be struck by such strong electrical charges that they could melt. Nowadays, lines made of synthetic fibre are used. Although they are stronger and lighter than the old kind of lines, they are not totally safe – especially in wet conditions.

The safe, stable Hargrave Box kite led to an increase in man-lifting attempts. The famous kite maker B.F.S. Baden-Powell succeeded in lifting an aerial to a height of 100m (325ft) above the ocean. This aerial allowed Guglielmo Marconi to carry out his equally famous experiments in wireless telegraphy.

The Parafoil is a wing which is made entirely of fabric. It has no rigid structure or frame. Its ventral fins provide stability.

Parafoils

Parafoils have an exceptional lifting capacity. They are capable of lifting photographic equipment, meteorological instruments or even people. They have no rigid structure and take their shape from the action of the wind.

In 1963, Domina Jalbert, an American who lived in Florida, designed the Parafoil. It was a kite which was perfect from the point of view of aerodynamics and was also very basic in terms of construction.

The Flexifoil is a stunt wing kite which can reach speeds of more than 100kph (62mph).

The kite takes its shape from the air, which flows inside the wing through its front edges, which are closed by a net with a large mesh.

The photograph shows the tail of a kite which takes shape when it is inflated by the wind. "Blow Fish", designed by Peter Lynn, New Zealand.

During international kite conventions, the skies are filled with spectacular kites in many different shapes and sizes – octopuses, flying saucers, hot air balloons, sharks, birds or even legs.

Delta Wing kites

These kites can fly in extremely light winds. They are based on Rogallo's Flexible kite. Francis Rogallo, an American aeronautical engineer, patented his flexible kite design in 1948. The dihedral wing and the keel mean that the kite is very stable. It adapts easily to variations in wind speed and direction.

Delta Wing kite.

A Malaysian Fighting Kite.

Fighting kites

These kites have a single towline. They move quickly in the direction indicated by their handler.

During fighting competitions, handlers try to cut the towlines of their opponents' kites. During kite festivals, however, unwanted accidents are often caused when the kites' lines get tangled up in each other.

The Wau Bulan kite is the best-known kite in Malaysia. It is also called the 'moon kite'. Its covering is richly decorated with fringes of coloured paper. It has no tail. Instead, it has a buzzer (a piece of split bamboo) which is fixed into the front. When it flies, it traces a flat figure of eight in the sky

After the Second World War, an American aeronautical engineer called Francis Rogallo designed a revolutionary kite. Its exceptional characteristics of lift and stability attracted the interest of NASA. In fact, NASA's programme for the parachutes which braked their spaceships was based on the Flexible kite. In the 1970s the Flexible kite gave rise to another project – the development of directional parachutes and, with the addition of a rigid structure, the Deltaplane. The Flexible kite has no rigid structure and is kept open by the power of the wind. Its shape and stability are provided by a series of vertical fins to which the towlines are hooked.

The Delta (see page 64) was based on the model with the rigid structure. It is similar to the Deltaplane, and has excellent qualities of lift and stability.

Figurative kites

The Butterfly is a light kite that is very common in China. The Thai Peacock kite is made of a head that waves in the air, so that when it flies its movement is similar to the writhing of a snake.

The Balinese Butterfly and Bat have bamboo frames and fabric coverings. The heads of the kites are made of papier-mâché and look very realistic.

The Parrot kite is found commonly in Brazil while in Japan, the Japanese term 'Mikawu Abu' means horsefly or gadfly. It is a splendid insect kite that provides an excuse for creating kites that make buzzing and humming sounds.

Other wonderful figurative kites are the Bee, the Hawk, the Mosquito and the Aeroplane, all of which combine fantastic visual effects with efficient aerodynamic qualities.

The great attention to detail that is lavished on figurative kites even results in the faithful reproduction of the movement of the creature or object depicted.

This kite depicts Saint Mark's Lion, the emblem of Venice.

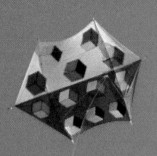

The north wind is a cold, usually dry, wind which blows from the north and brings clear skies and a drop in temperature. This wind blows in strong gusts.
In ancient times, it was called the Boreas or Aquilone – the cause of earthquakes and the kidnapper of young girls.
It was depicted as an old man with a beard and a seashell in his hand – maybe as a symbol of the sound the north wind made when it blew.
The old man wore a swirling cloak which raised flurries of snow and dust. A 'snake's tail' emerging from under the cloak, was seen as an indication of lightning.

Above: A Sanjo Rokkaku kite flying at high altitude. In the photograph below – a cellular kite (Star box).

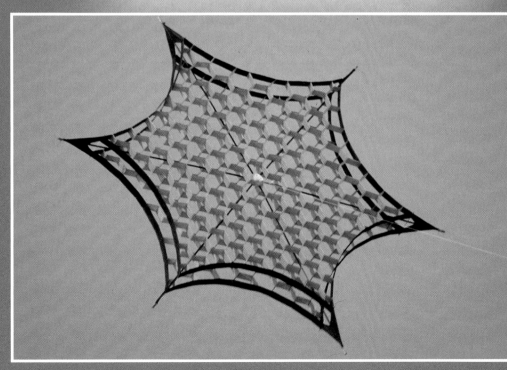

The best place for kite building is a big room with plenty of light. You will need a large worktable – especially if you intend to build large kites.

You will need pencils, a ruler, a set square, a sharp pair of scissors, a cutter, a saw, a 1m (3ft 3in) rule, a fabric puncher, a pair of pliers, glue, adhesive tape, needles, nylon thread, kitchen string, nails, screws and screwdrivers, a drill, sandpaper and a file.

Some statistics

The longest kite measuring 714.2m/2,342ft was called Arturo. It was built in Perugia, Italy, and launched for the first time on 1 July 1986.

The altitude record for a single kite of 3,801m/12,467ft was set on 28 February 1898 at a weather station in Massachusetts, USA.

The highest altitude for a train of kites of 9,740m/31,947ft was reached on 1 August 1919 in Lindenberg, Germany.

The fastest kite, a Flexifoil, was launched on 22 September 1989 in Maryland, USA. It reached a speed of 193kph (120mph), measured using the local police radar speed-trap system.

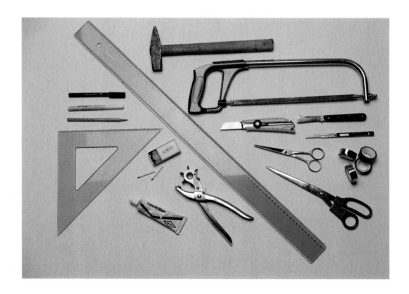

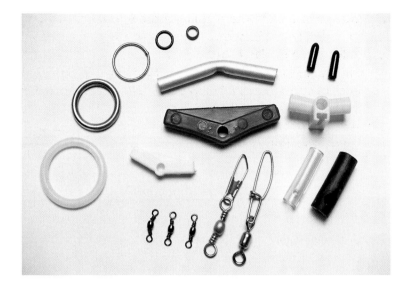

Rings   Plastic or metal rings are useful for joining bridles and towlines. They are better than string, as they avoid knots, which have a tendency to be difficult to undo, so that you need a pair of scissors to free them.

Joints   A variety of hard plastic joints is needed – T, V, Y, cross-joints and straight joints. They are used for joining longerons, or spines, and traverses, or spars.

Tubing   Plastic or rubber tubing is used for joining longerons and traverses or covering a frame. It is a cost-effective and simple alternative to connections or attachments which could otherwise be complicated to carry out.

Tips   These plastic points are inserted onto the end of tapered rods.

Thimble   This is a ring made of plastic or metal for reinforcing an eyelet in the covering – for example, where the towline has to be attached.

Tie rod   A metal element that can hold a line which is attached to it. It functions like a buckle on a belt, or pair of braces.

Winding reel   This is provided with a spring catch and a metal snap hook that are linked by means of a ring and a spool. When the towline is hooked to the ring attached to the bridle, the line can turn freely.

The frame

Different kinds of materials are necessary for constructing kites. These materials vary according to the size of the kite and the kind of performance required from it – such as flying altitude, durability, or carrying various kinds of scientific instruments.

Rounded sticks are used for constructing kites. They are generally 0.1–1cm (1/32–3/8in) in diameter and 1–1.5m (3–5ft) in length, although they can be as long as 2m (6ft).

One of the most important features is **lightness**. Three sticks or rods of the same size (diameter 0.6cm/1/4in, length 1m/3ft) made of a light wood, such as rattan, carbon and fibreglass respectively vary considerably in weight - the rattan stick weighs 15g (1/2oz), the carbon rod weighs 16g (9/16oz), and the fibreglass rod weighs 35g (11/4oz).

Although rattan would seem to be ideal as it is so light, its bending **strength** must also be taken into account. The bending strength of rattan is three times less than that of carbon fibre, while fibreglass has no equal in terms of flexibility, despite its heavier weight.

Some kites, such as fighting kites, need to be very flexible so that they can adapt to the thrust of the wind. On the other hand, box or cellular kites must have a rigid structure that does not bend. With these, the correct balance between the support surfaces and the stabilizing surfaces must always be maintained.

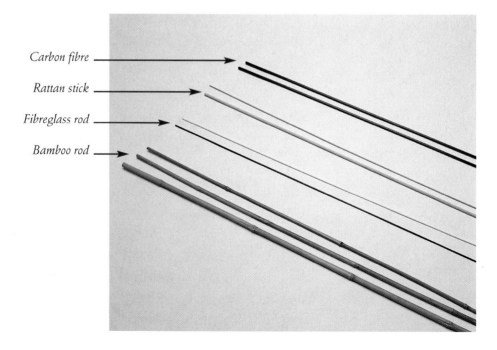

Carbon fibre

Rattan stick

Fibreglass rod

Bamboo rod

Bamboo is very strong, flexible and easy to work with. It is thus the most frequently used material in kite construction, and is pretty much irreplaceable in the construction of figurative kites.

Rattan sticks are light and have a uniform shape. They are ideal for constructing static flyer kites with a specific, well-defined symmetrical shape. (Lozenge or Diamond kite, see page 50, or Square kite, see page 70).

The most advanced kites, such as stunt kites, must have extremely strong, rigid support structures made of **carbon fibre**. This material is extremely light, as well as being resistant to different kinds of stress, such as bending, compression or torsion.

A hacksaw is needed for cutting rods made of fibreglass, carbon fibre or sticks of bamboo. A cutter or knife is necessary for slicing into rattan or small pieces of bamboo.

Finally, the frame of a kite is completed by framing lines, or bridle lines, which must be strong, light and inflexible.

Nylon fishing line or twisted nylon line are good alternatives, but if you want to build kites of extremely high quality it is better to use alternative materials like Dacron or Kevlar.

A splendid figurative kite with a bamboo frame.

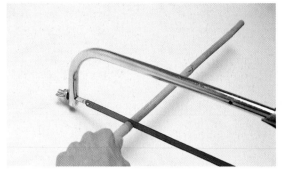

Working with bamboo

Bamboo is one of the best materials for making kite frames. It is strong, flexible and easy to work with.

Use a hacksaw to cut the bamboo, as the cane is very hard.

Hold the bamboo in your hand, rather than putting it in a vice. This will avoid fracturing the cane along its length.

Make a precise cut by moving the hacksaw back and forth.

Later, the bamboo can be cut into sections along its length. Use a knife with a strong blade, like a carpet cutter or Stanley knife.

Move the blade along the fibre of the cane.

The nodes are the most difficult points to cut through. Be careful not to cut yourself. Although the nodes are very hard, they can spring open suddenly when cut with a sharp blade.

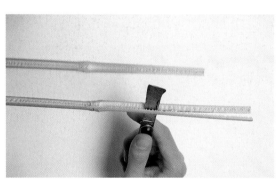

The half sections of cane can be divided again to obtain very thin sticks, depending on the size that you need.

Use the blade of the cutter to smooth the edges of the sticks. This will make them even lighter, but will not weaken them.

Bamboo

Bamboo is the Malaysian name for an extremely strong plant which grows in cane groves along the banks of rivers or in swamps. It is used in native medicine, in the building and transport industries, for making furniture, decorations and fans.

Bending the rods

Bamboo is extremely flexible. It bends under pressure, but returns to its original shape when the pressure is released. If you want the bamboo to be permanently curved, you should treat it with heat. This bending technique is essential if you want to build figurative kites.

Use a candle flame to heat the parts of the rod that you want to bend. Move the cane close to the flame, but be careful not to burn yourself.

Hold the rod firmly, then begin to flex it.

Keep rotating the bamboo over the flame.

When the bamboo has assumed the shape that you want, keep holding it over the flame in order to fix it into its new shape.

Martin Lester

Martin Lester is an English kite-maker who builds traditional kites as well as windsocks made of spinnaker fabric. Some examples of his work are the Eagle, the Goose, the Stork, the Shark, the Shuttle and the Pink Flamingo.

Sails or covering

The sails or covering of a kite must be very light, with a low level of porosity. In fact, if you use a light but porous fabric your kite will be light – but it will not be very good at flying. This is because the air that passes through the sails or covering will not give the kite any lift.

The Chinese used to use silk for making kites, but it was very expensive. This meant that only a few rich people were able to experience the pleasure of kite flying.

This problem was resolved when paper was invented. Instead of silk, the sails or covering were made of parchment – a lightweight paper with a low level of porosity.

Working with paper is not only simple, but also very quick. The different pieces can be stuck together with repeated applications of glue, which can also be used to strengthen those parts of the covering that are subject to pressure or stress.

On the other hand, paper kites tear very easily. They are ruined by rain or damp weather and they cannot be dismantled for storage or repairs.

Despite all this, figurative kites and fighting kites are still made of paper and bamboo.

Sails or coverings made of spinnaker fabric or Tyvek are ideal for kites that have frames made of fibreglass or carbon fibre.

Tissue paper can be bought in stationery shops. Spinnaker fabric is available in specialist model shops or at kite conventions.

Another good alternative material for these kinds of kites is nylon, as it has a low level of porosity and is highly resistant both to damp conditions and wear and tear.

Spinnaker fabric is essential if you intend to build stunt kites. Traditional materials cannot withstand the constant stress and wear and tear to which these advanced types of kites are subjected.

Sails or coverings must be made and fitted with exact precision, otherwise the kite will not be balanced correctly.

When making sails or coverings, check the sizes and measurements again and again. Before you cut the fabric, check the weave and make sure that it is straight.

Hem the sides of the fabric. This will confer extra strength and ensure that stretching is reduced.

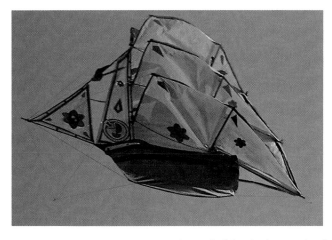

A wonderful sailer kite made of paper and bamboo by Medio Calderoni.

Fabric sails or coverings

Sails and coverings for large kites are made of fabric because it is strong – if your large kite falls to the ground, you have a good chance of finding it still in one piece. Fabric is also easy to dismantle, so kites made of it are easy to transport.

Nowadays, the most common materials are Tyvek and spinnaker nylon. Tyvek is easily glued with synthetic glue, or it can be stitched without any problems. Spinnaker nylon can also be sewn.

When you want to cut out sails from nylon, you should use a hot soldering iron and a metal ruler for guiding it along the right line.

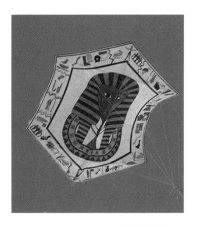

The Sanjo Rokkaku kite – the fighting kite used in competitions in Japan.

Small scraps of fabric were sewn together to make this brightly coloured covering for a Delta kite.

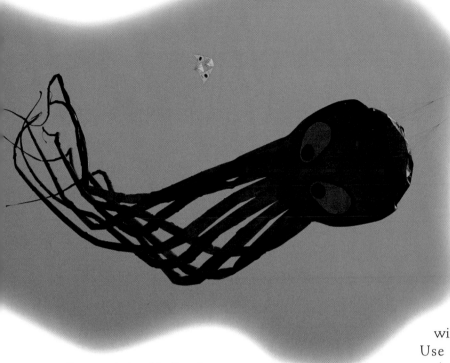

Octopus, designed by Peter Lynn.

This method will stop the material curling or fraying, and will also mean that you can solder together different coloured pieces of decorative material.

When attempting more ambitious patterns, you should first make a template from wrapping paper, which is idea for this purpose, as it is very rigid. Then put the template onto the material and fix it in place with sewing pins.

Use nails to fix the sail fabric onto a sheet of plywood. Make sure that the fabric is stretched tight.

Lift and stability

The horizontal sail surface of a kite confers lift. This has nothing to do with the stability which is created by tails of different shapes and sizes. Many kites achieve stable flight without the use of a tail because they use vertical sails that confer stability (see page 64). A horizontal surface has 100 per cent lift and 0 per cent stability.

On the other hand, a vertical surface has 0 per cent lift and 100 per cent stability. In order to understand the lift of a surface which is positioned at an angle, it is necessary to estimate its horizontal and vertical projection. A surface angled at 45° will have the same degree of lift and stability.

Look at Medio Calderoni's Sailing Ship kite on page 100 and note the support parts of the three sails and the stabilizing element provided by the vertical triangular sail – or the mainsail of the sailing ship. On the other hand, because the hull is at an angle, it combines both these functions in different proportions. The slight angle of the three sails increases the overall stability of the kite.

If you fold a flat Lozenge, or Diamond, kite in the centre (see page 50) using a V joint, you will find yourself with a kite with good stability, due to the small angle of inclination.

Then use tailor's chalk to draw around the outline. Leave a margin that is sufficient for any flaps, folds, pocket fastenings or junctions which might be necessary.

Mark the template precisely at the points where the sails or covering need cuts, openings and holes to pass the bridle or tow lines through. Also mark the points where the frame will be joined to the sail or covering.

Use a sharp pair of scissors to cut the fabric, or a cutter with an aluminium ruler to guide it.

Your sewing machine should be able to regulate the size of the sewing stitches, and to reverse the direction of the seam without your having to turn all the fabric around. You should use thread of a type which is similar to the fabric, so that it undergoes the same wear and tear as the sail or covering from the effect of heat and rain. Sew a seam along the free edges and add a strip of fabric to strengthen them – you might find that it is rather difficult to position the strengthening strip of fabric correctly under the needle.

Machine-sew the fabric sails or covering using 100 per cent polyester thread and sharp size 75–80 needles. You will also need needles for hand sewing and sewing pins for fixing the sail or covering when cutting or working with the fabric.

Use a hot knife (similar to a soft soldering iron) or a pair of scissors to cut spinnaker fabric.

Everything you need for making a fabric sail or covering. 100 per cent polyester thread, sewing needles, pins, sewing thimble, coloured chalk and tailor's chalk, felt and ballpoint pens, and different sizes of sewing elastic.

Porosity

The kind of fabric used for the sails or covering will determine the level of porosity – ie the quantity of air which passes through the sails or covering. If the air cannot pass through the fabric it creates pressure which is transformed into an upward thrust. So kites that are made of waterproof material lift rapidly and respond quickly to their handler's commands. Kites with sails or covering made of cotton or linen – fabrics that have a large weave – can only fly in strong winds, and such kites must also be of a considerable size. Spinnaker fabric, paper and silk have a low level of porosity, which makes them ideal for making kites. Plastic and polythene shopping bags are not porous, so they are a cost-effective alternative for making sails or coverings.

A kite based on the Multiflare design.

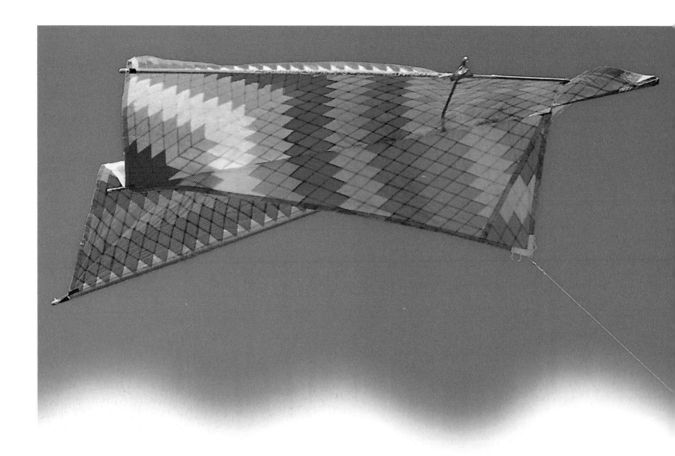

A Delta Kite.

Decoration

The art of decorating kites dates back to ancient times. The sails or coverings are painted with designs that can be seen from far away.

Decorations on paper

The first thing to do is to choose the kind of colour medium that is most suitable for the surface you are going to decorate.

You should use felt pens with different-sized tips on tissue paper or other kinds of thin paper. Tempera or acrylic pens work well on thicker paper. Experience is required to decorate with felt pens, but they can create very effective designs in different colours.

Paper can also be decorated with other pieces of different-coloured paper. Even people who are not very good at art can create effective designs by using this method. You should use coloured tissue paper, gift-wrapping paper or pieces cut out of newspapers or magazines.

Bear in mind that you should not weigh down the kite too much.

Decorations on fabric

Decorating fabric is an ancient art. People used to decorate fighting kites with frightening images to terrify their opponents. On other kites, symbols of happiness and prosperity were depicted to bring good luck.

You should use a waterproof colour medium when decorating fabric. Spinnaker fabric only comes in plain colours. In order to decorate it, you should sew other pieces of coloured fabric onto it. When you see a beautifully decorated kite flying in the air, remember that it has taken its owner a lot of time and imagination to create it.

A big Sanjo Rokkaku kite with sails made of spinnaker fabric. The decorations have been sewn on using a technique similar to patchwork.

Use a patchwork technique if you want to create geometrical patterns. Join the pieces of fabric with a seam 0.6cm (1/4in) from the edge, and then turn them over and attach them to the back of the sail with another seam.

If you leave a larger margin, you will strengthen the design, but in this case you should sew two seams to attach the fabric to the kite. This is always necessary when decorating stunt kites.

Make sure that you do not weigh down the kite too much, and take care to ensure that the right side of the fabric is in view when the kite is being flown.

If you want to create a non-geometrical design, use a single sail as a base and use a felt pen to draw the design you want.

Select pieces of fabric in different colours and attach them to the sail with sewing pins, following the design you have already drawn. Then sew the seams, attaching the pieces of fabric to the sail.

You can decorate either the front or the back of the kite. You should try and imagine the effect you want to create when the kite is in the air.

Trim the excess fabric 0.3cm (¹/₈in) from the seam. Turn the fabric over and cut along the main sail inside the design you have sewn. Proceed in the same way until you have finished the decoration you want to create.

You do not have to cut the fabric of the main sail if the piece of fabric you are using is white.

Spaceship –
this kite has no frame.

A Japanese legend states that a samurai, who was exiled to the island of Hachijo with his son, decided to build a kite which would be big enough to carry the boy back to the mainland. Since that time – the 12th century – all Hachijo kites have been decorated with the face of that young boy.

In Japan, competitions are held every year using fighting kites decorated with the traditional colours and insignia of their area of origin.

Another story tells that when a boy called Kintaro (the golden boy) was abandoned in a forest, he was found and brought up by a family of bears. He became the strongest boy in the land. When kites were given to newborn baby boys, they were decorated with an image of Kintaro's face and covered with good-luck messages that would keep away evil spirits and attract the favour of the gods who protected children.

Sicilian Diamond kites are famous. They were built to welcome King Humbert I and Queen Margaret of Italy, and were decorated with images of the sovereigns' faces.

On page 31

Elisa is flying a pretty, coloured kite which is based on the Delta. The sail surface has been increased by lengthening the longeron, or spine.

In the Orient, kite makers are more concerned with the colours of their kites and the decorations on them than with how efficient they are at flying.

These kite makers are particularly interested in how the kite moves when it is in the air. A fish-shaped kite should appear to swim. A snake should appear to slither. A large man should move slowly and heavily. In the West, however, kite makers are more concerned with their kites' efficiency and capacity of movement, rather than with beautiful decorations – although more recently, examples of beautifully decorated kites have become more common.

Assembling your kite

Each component – rods, sails, bridles, joints and fastenings – must be carefully assembled so that you create a light, strong kite.

You should make sure that the sails or covering are reinforced at the points which might be subject to tearing or stress. This will ensure that the connections between the various parts are strong and secure. Use strong material, or several layers of the same material either glued or sewn together. Use adhesive tape to strengthen paper at critical points.

Use Dacron – a hardwearing synthetic material – for the spinnaker. Where you want to attach the rods, make a pocket fastening which is long enough to distribute the stress imposed by the structure of the sails or covering along its entire length. The pocket fastening should be made of the same material as the sails or covering, and it should be reinforced around the edges.

You should make sure that the ends of the rods do not break the material. So it is a good idea to round off the ends and protect them with a piece of adhesive tape. You could also cover them with a rubber tip.

Sew some elastic into the ends of the pocket fastenings in such a way as to ensure that the rods inside are kept firmly in place. This also means that it is easier to replace the rods when they get broken. (see p. 33, figs. 2-3).

When you use joints for connecting parts of the frame, check that the holes in them are of the same diameter as the rods. If the holes are too big, the rods might break or split at the point of contact.

When you have to attach rods to sails or coverings made of spinnaker fabric, connect some rubber tubing to a strip of the same fabric as the sail – or Dacron will do – which should be sewn onto the sail itself. This makes it easier to dismantle the kites and replace the rods.

Finally, be very careful when connecting the bridles to the frame to make sure that the sails or covering do not tear. You should also make sure that the movement of the lines does not inflict any wear or tear on the material. It is a good idea to reinforce the passing holes with an extra seam, or with some adhesive tape.

A cellular Box kite.

Connections and fastenings

1   *The sails or coverings are kept taut by a rubber tube that is held in place by a cord. The rod that keeps the sail open is housed inside the rubber tube.*

2–3   *Sew some elastic onto the end of the pocket fastening so that it is easier to replace the rods.*

4   *This fastening is used to attach the longeron or spine to the traverse or spar. The connecting element is a tube made of perforated rubber which is inserted into the longeron.*

5-6   *Details of connections used for stunt kites.*

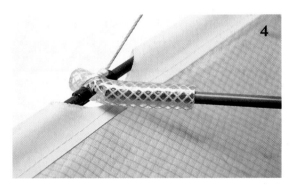

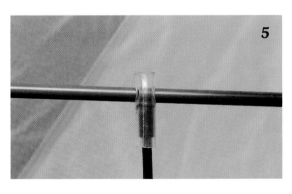

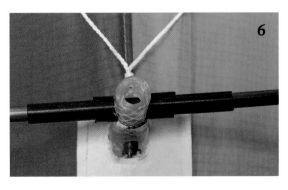

Bridles

A Sanjo Rokkaku kite in flight.

A kite with a modified Sanjo Rokkaku frame.

Bridles can be made of one or two lines. This depends on the type of kite, its size and the materials from which it is made.

The bridle is made of up a series of lines that keep the kite in the right shape. It allows the kite to rise with the thrust of the wind and to fly between the air currents in a balanced fashion. You should carry out a few tests in order to decide on the length of the bridle and the point at which the towline should be attached. Block the bridle in place only when you have discovered the right attack angle for your kite.

When you are in your car, try putting your hand out of the window. You will feel the pressure of the wind on it. Move your hand until you can split the wind – your hand will feel weightless. This means that you have found the best attack angle in relation to wind and speed.

If the towline is attached directly to the frame of your kite (Box, Crate or Snowflake kites), it is not possible to change the flying arrangement.

The bridle stops the kite frame from bending out of shape. Some very large kites are bridled with hundreds of lines.

The bridle should not be too long, as in this case it will lose tension easily, which makes it difficult to control the kite when it is in the air. On the other hand, if a bridle is too short it will reduce the stability of the kite.

A bridle with two lines is fixed to the longeron or spine. The kite should not be bridled until it has been completely constructed and decorated.

The fastening points for the bridle weaken the frame of the kite. They erode wood and can tear the sails or covering, so it is a good idea to strengthen the passing holes, with adhesive tape if the kite is made of paper, or with scraps of fabric sewn around the passing holes if the kite is made of fabric.

If you are making a Diamond kite (see page 50), fix one end of the bridle to the end of the longeron or spine at the front of the kite. Tie the other end halfway between the point where the rods cross and the end of the longeron or spine.

Fix a strong ring to the bridle at the point which corresponds to the length of the main rod. If the first part of the bridle is too long, the attack angle is too big. This means that the kite will not rise. If the attack angle is too small, the kite will vibrate and flutter wildly in the air.

You can shorten or lengthen the sections of the bridle by moving the ring back and forth along it until you have found the perfect configuration.

A huge Sanjo Rokkaku kite.

Bearing strength *is the capacity of a material to support a load without changing shape. Bamboo, fibreglass and carbon fibre have good bearing strength.*

Bending strength *is the capacity to support perpendicular pressure along a longitudinal axis without undergoing a change in shape. Bamboo and carbon fibre have the best bending strength.*

Elasticity *or flexibility is the capacity to bend without breaking. The most elastic materials are bamboo and solid fibreglass. Wood is more fragile, as it is so rigid.*

Attach the bridle to the towline with a lark's head hitch or cow hitch, so that you do not have to keep tying and untying the knots.

Tails

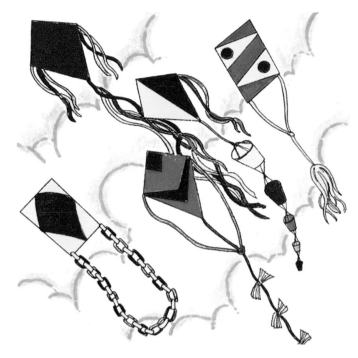

Brightly coloured and strangely shaped tails capture the imagination. A simple strip of material can be transformed into piano keys, a metre rule, a snake or the notes of a musical stave…

Sometimes a kite will rise but then lose height after reaching a certain altitude. It begins to turn around and fall towards the ground. Nothing can be done except to pick it up again and regulate the bridle.

Some kites, such as flat or plane surface kites, need a stabilizing tail. In other kites, the tail acts as a kind of rudder because it improves flying quality and response to changes in wind direction.

If there is a strong wind, the tail flies horizontally. This means that it generates a tractive force that makes the kite adopt a low attack angle, which reduces resistance and increases stability.

On the other hand, if the wind drops, the weight of the tail will pull the kite down. This means that the sails can receive more wind and lift will be improved.

The fastening point of the tail to the kite determines its function. The tail acts according to the principle of the action of a lever. One arm represents the distance from the barycentre of the kite and the other the length of the tail itself. Another function of the tail is that it confers inertial force. When the wind makes the kite go out of control, so that it performs a series of swerving movements, the tail acts as a kind of shock absorber.

Sirocco

This is a hot wind that blows across the Mediterranean from the southeast, bringing rain with it.

Different kinds of tails

- **Stabilizing tails** (for flat or plane surface kites). This kind of tail is made of strips of material of 2-11m (6–36ft), which should be attached to the end of the central longeron or spine.

- Thread rectangles of accordion-pleated paper onto a line – they will create considerable resistance. Adjust the length and the distance between the **bows** of paper.

- A **ring** tail will create even greater resistance.

- A series of **tapering cones** will create even more resistance than the alternatives described above. They should be linked to each other at a distance of 20–30cm (8–12in). When the air enters the upper opening it creates pressure and friction inside the cone. This means that it has to change speed and strong disturbance is produced at the exit point. This kind of tail can be made by cutting the bottoms off plastic drinking glasses.

No one can predict the wind conditions that will occur at a flying site. For this reason, it is a good idea to make sure that you are always equipped with different kinds of tails.

A fantastic Delta kite in flight. The tube-shaped tail is fixed to the towline.

Parafoil.

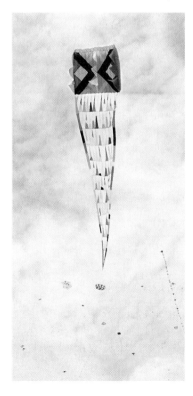

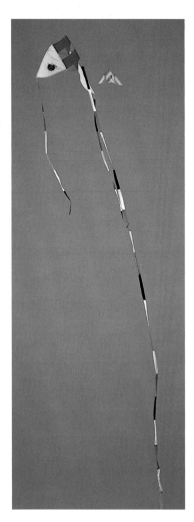

Fringed tails, which lend a pleasing visual effect as well as increasing the stabilizing function of the kite.

In order to create a pleasing visual effect, other kinds of imaginative tails can be hooked to the towline. In this case, however, the kite must have good lifting power to be able to carry the extra weight.

The most suitable kites for this method are the Delta (see page 64) and the Conyne (see page 82).

Use a pulley or spring catch to connect the tail to the towline, so that it can move freely.

Delta Box Kite with long tubular tails.

A detail of the tail fastening. The pulley, or spring catch, is attached to the frame in order to preventing the tail from getting tangled up – which can be very irritating.

A Delta Box Kite with a multicoloured tail.

Towlines

The towline serves to anchor the kite to the ground, but its characteristics also influence the kite's quality of flight.

The principal function of a towline is that it should provide tractive force. This is because it is continually subjected to stress and tension due to the force of the wind.

You should calculate the tractive force and multiply it by two in order to decide on the diameter of the line you want to use. The result should correspond to the degree of resistance that the line is capable of. It is not always possible to assess the power of a kite, because it can vary in relation to the type of wind in which it is being flown. In addition, when you buy lines you will find that the packaging does not always give any indication of their break strength.

The flexibility of the line does not have any great influence on the quality of flight, but it does have a bearing on unwinding and rewinding. As far as stunt kites are concerned, however, flexibility can affect the kite's response time to its handler's commands.

If the towline has a large diameter, it can present an obstacle to the kite as it rises into the air. In fact, if you multiply the thickness of the line by its length, you will find that the overall area is quite considerable. In addition, when air hits the line, the latter does not stay perfectly taut – it bends as a result of its own weight combined with the friction caused by the wind.

Above: A Delta kite with a wind turbine hooked to the towline. The wind turbine is purely decorative.

Various kinds of lines that can be used as towlines.

The Delta kite is probably the safest and most stable of kites. Its lifting capacity is such that it is possible to hook wonderful windsocks to the towline.

A kite that is capable of lifting 200g (7oz) cannot fly if it has a towline that weighs double that weight.

You should buy at least three different kinds of lines to use in relation to different kinds of wind conditions. In general, lines made of twisted synthetic thread – such as nylon – are used. Lines made of metal should be avoided.

Hook the line to the bridle ring, using a fishing hook with a pulley or spring catch. This will ensure that the towline does not get tangled up.

As nylon lines tend to play out quickly, you should wear gloves to make sure that your hands do not suffer any rope burns or other injuries.

You can send tissue paper parachutes or bags of coriander to a considerable height with messenger kites (see page 138). They can be detached from the towline by means of a small contraption and then fall slowly to the ground.

Knots

Knots are extremely important and very helpful, connecting parts of the frame to the sails or covering, to the bridle and to the towline. A well-tied knot is easy to undo without having to resort to a pair of scissors.

In general, the lines used for kites are made of synthetic material. Those made of 100 per cent polyester or other fibres have a lot of advantages – but they can be very slippery, and can also have a tendency to loosen very easily.

A badly tied knot can cut the towline or change the arrangement of the bridle. The right kind of knot does not come undone at the wrong moment – nor does it loosen in a dangerous manner.

It is therefore important to know about the various different characteristics of knots – and to master the technique of tying them.

A variation of the Sanjo Rokkaku kite.

*The most common kind of knot is the **bowline***.

Step 1

Step 2

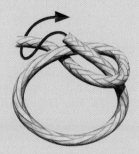

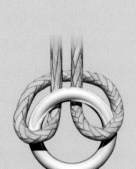

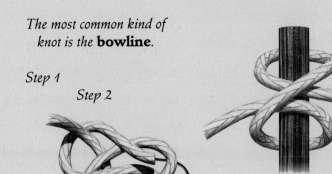

A clove hitch
Tied around a rod or spar.

*A **lark's head hitch or cow hitch**. When the bridle is being made, a ring with this kind of knot should be positioned at the point to which the towline is to be attached. This is useful when the kite is being tested to find the best possible arrangement.*

Sheet bend *or* **common bend**, *used for connecting lines of different diameters.*

Reef *knot or* **flat** *knot*

*The **Dutch Marine bowline or Cowboy bowline** knot is a very safe and reliable knot. It can be used during construction and in flight. As it is not a slipknot, it is easy to undo.*

Winding reels

Winding reels are used for launching – and above all, retrieving – kites.

Winding reels are used for winding in the towline. Their winding capacity – ie their capacity to lengthen and shorten the line – is an essential factor of a successful flight.

The stability of a kite, in fact, depends on the towline being held taut all the time. If the line slackens, the kite begins to sway and then drop towards the ground.

There are many kinds of winding reels – from simple handles, through yo-yos, to sophisticated spools with reduction gears.

If you need to control a two-line stunt kite, you should use two spool-handles, called yo-yos. Select your winding reel in relation to the strength of the wind, the size of your kite and the altitude you want it to reach. If you want to fly your kite very high, you should use a reel with a crank handle, as it can hold a lot of line.

If your kite is high and there is a lot of wind, you should use a strong reel equipped with a good converter – a chain drive or gear transmission device, which serves to reduce the speed.

If you want to fly a small kite at a low altitude, ie no more than 100m (325ft), use a simple piece of wood cut into the shape of an H or a yo-yo. The yo-yo is an ideal option, as it runs easily between the fingers and plays out the line very quickly.

If you want to fly a fighting kite, do not use a winding reel – control it directly via the towlines. It is inevitable that some of the line will end up on the ground, so be careful not to get tangled up in it and fall over. When the battle is over, wind the line back onto the reel immediately.

The evolution of stunt kites (see page 114) controlled via one or two bars has been due to the movement of the arms and wrists. The towlines are connected to the ends of the bars, around which they are rewound once the flying session is finished.

A winding reel with an extension similar to a short fishing rod can make a kite fly in very little wind, with the right kind of jerking action on the line. You should always remember to connect the beginning of the line firmly to the reel – otherwise you risk seeing your kite fly away on the wind, with no means of controlling it!

Kite construction

*Making kites is an art, a technique,
a lot of work, a hobby –
and a kind of game.*

Recreation kites

*The simplest kind of kite originated in Peru –
where it is called the Chiringa.
It is made by folding a sheet of paper. Hooded or
arch-top kites are even more enjoyable.*

Hooded or arch-top kites

The purple kite here has been made from a strip of paper, which has been rolled into the shape of a cone in the centre and fixed with glue or staples. The yellow kite has been made from a rectangle that has been folded at the top end – the points of the corners have been joined together. If you want to make a lively kind of tail, use strips of crinkled coloured paper.

The bridle of each of these kites should be made with a single line, which should be fixed firmly to the kite with a few metal staples.

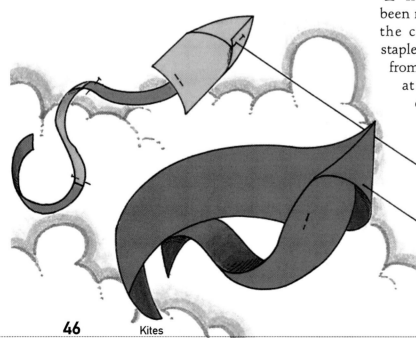

The Chiringa

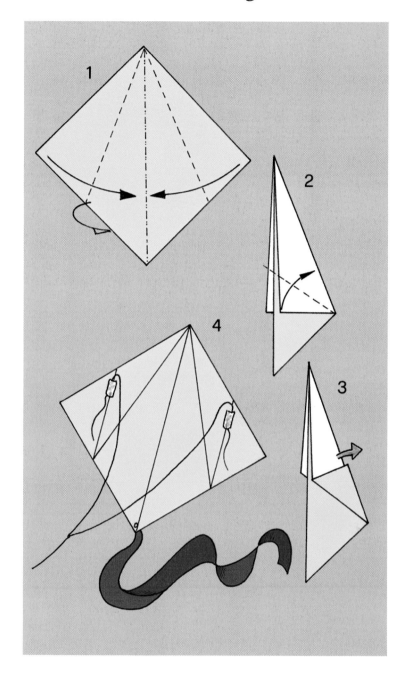

*According to tradition,
the March wind heralds
a change of season.
It brings plants to life
and carries rain with it.*

1 *Cut out a square of paper and fold it as indicated in 1, 2
and 3 above.*

2 *Use adhesive tape to fix a 60cm (2ft) long bridle at the points
shown in 4 above.*

3 *Knot the towline in the middle of the bridle.*

4 *Make the tail with a strip of paper 3–4m (10–13ft) long and
3m (10ft) wide – then wait for the wind!*

The Dragon

This kite can be made with a sheet of A4 typing paper (29.7 x 21cm/11³/₄ x 8¹/₄in).

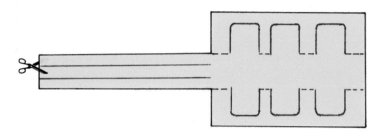

Cut the paper into the shape indicated above, then cut along the red lines and fold as indicated by the dotted lines above.

Insert the frame, which should be made of thin, light wooden splines, following the black dotted lines above.

The bridle is made of strong sewing thread. It should be fixed to the first and last openings, as shown above.

Take a sheet of newspaper

The sails or covering are made by folding a piece of paper – even a sheet of newspaper – as indicated in the diagram below.

You can decorate this kite with fringes or streamers. You can also make holes in it and stick coloured pieces of tissue paper behind the openings you have made.

The frame is made of two limewood rods 0.3cm (¹/₈in) wide and 0.2cm (³/₃₂in) high.

Make the tail with a strip of newspaper 2m (6ft) long – you can attach shorter strips to it.

Attach the bridle at the point where the longeron or spine crosses the traverse, and at the rear of the longeron.

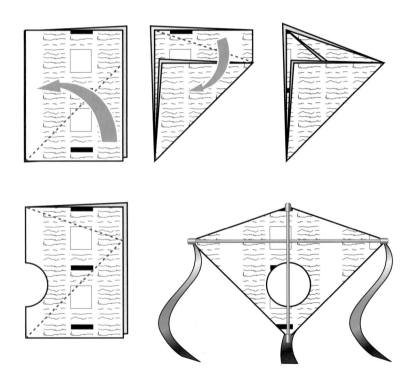

When the air is very clear and it is possible to see a long way off, it means that atmospheric disturbances are on the way. If there is a fresh breeze in the air, it means that it has been raining somewhere near, and that rain is on the way.

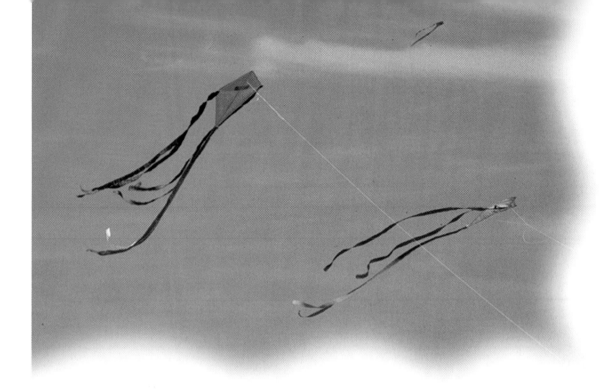

Lozenge or Diamond kites

The Lozenge or Diamond kite is the typical symbol of kites. It is easy to make and has good flying qualities. The frame is made of two rods – wingspan and longeron, or spine. The sails or covering can be made of paper, fabric or polythene. The tails are made of strips 2–3cm (³/₄–1¹/₈in) wide and 2–11m (6–36ft) long.

The Diamond kite can reach high altitudes in a short time, with steady wind conditions. It is an extremely satisfying kite to fly.

The Diamond is a flat, or plane surface, kite. It needs a tail to maintain stability. You should use a classic ring tail, or a tail with bows, which is able to combat the wind.

As long as you maintain the correct proportions, you can make this kind of kite as big as you like. Do not, however, underestimate its power, as it is capable of lifting considerable weights.

The Diamond kite can fly in very light winds (as low as 3kph/1.8mph), but it remains stable in winds as fast as 30kph (18mph).

You should use a strong towline.

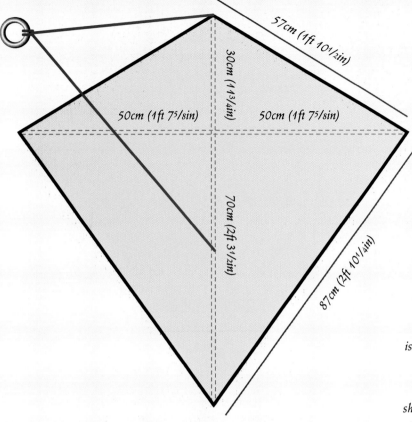

57cm (1ft 10¹/₂in)

30cm (11³/₄in)

50cm (1ft 7⁵/₈in) 50cm (1ft 7⁵/₈in)

70cm (2ft 3¹/₂in)

87cm (2ft 10¹/₄in)

You can use various materials to make the sails or covering – tissue paper, a sheet of newspaper, wrapping paper, or even a plastic rubbish bag.

Use a flexible rod for the traverse in order to increase the stability of the kite.

The length of the tail (at the sides and the lowest point) should be equal to seven times the length of the kite itself.

Shorten the tail in light wind conditions. Lengthen the tail when the wind is stronger.

The size of the kites shown here is rarely more than 1m (3ft). In fact, the rods available in shops are usually this size. If you want to increase the size of your kite, you should obviously make sure that you respect the correct proportions. On the other hand, you should not make the mistake of thinking that you will achieve a successful flight if you modify your kite in proportion in terms of length and width.

If you stray away from the traditional models – which have been tried and tested over time – you risk going through a long series of tests and attempts before achieving success.

There are certain rules which should be followed when you venture into making kites.

In general, a big kite is more easily launched and gains altitude with few problems. A big kite might be a little slow when you want to launch it, and you might need a friend to help you. On the other hand, big kites are more tolerant of faults in design.

A small kite, however, does not easily forgive any errors in design – and it could pay you back by being very difficult to launch into the air. Yet you should remember that once you have launched a small kite, it will give you a lot of satisfaction in terms of speed, response and stunts.

During the 1800s many inventors used kites as a means of saving people who were in danger of drowning. They had understood that the same wind that threw ships against dangerous rocks could be used to pull life rafts to the shore.

Making a Lozenge or Diamond Kite

Cut pieces of coloured tissue paper along the diagonal.

Stick them together with glue or, for a quicker alternative, use adhesive tape.

Position the vertical rod along the line that connects the two coloured sails and cut away any excess. Use adhesive tape to fix it vertically to the corners.

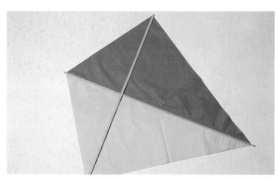

Fix the horizontal rod. Make sure that the paper stays taut and that the two sections are symmetrical in relation to each other.

Strengthen the inside edge of the sails with adhesive tape, to make sure that the kite does not tear.

Use adhesive tape to strengthen the corners.

Use adhesive tape to strengthen the outside edges of the kite to make sure that the sails do not tear.

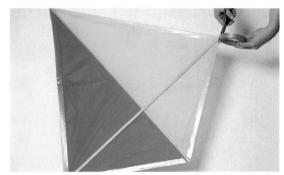

Use strong, wide adhesive tape to strengthen the corners. Make sure that it is firmly stuck to the rod.

About a third of the way down the longeron, strengthen the sails with adhesive tape. Attach the second bridle line at this point.

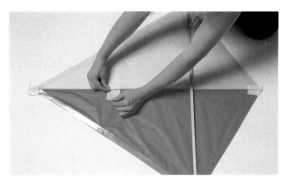

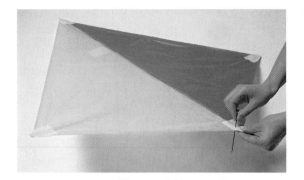

The bridle

Use a needle to thread the line through the sails and connect it to the upper part of the kite.

Secure the knot several times.

Pull the knot tight. The line should come out of the part that is opposite to the frame. This method means that the wind cannot tear the sails away from the rods.

Measure out a length of line that is equal to the entire perimeter of the kite and tie one end to the lower end of the kite.

The following diagrams illustrate three different bridle configurations.

Inside the surface of the kite.
Very strong wind.

Outside the surface of the kite.
Very light wind.

Slightly inside the surface of the kite.
Medium, steady wind.

The distance between the bridle knot and the surface of the kite must be greater than the width of the kite itself.

Attach the tail to the side edges and the lowest point of the kite.

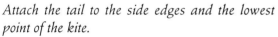

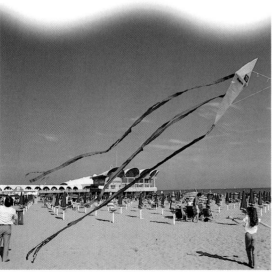

The Eddy kite

At the end of the 19th century an American journalist called William A. Eddy, who was fanatical about photography, was in search of a stable method that would be capable of carrying his photographic equipment to a certain altitude. At that time, the kite was the only alternative capable of satisfying his needs. The Lozenge, or Diamond, kite was not stable enough, and its tail would hamper the photographic equipment considerably. In 1891, Eddy designed a kite which was a modified version of the Diamond. He used a bender to curve the wingspan traverse. The sails formed a dihedral angle which rendered the kite stable – even without a tail. Eddy was able to take the first aerial photographs due to the considerable stability and lifting qualities of his kite.

The best wind for kite flying is a steady wind, as it will take the kite to a high altitude in a short time, giving the kite's handler a lot of enjoyment and satisfaction.

In 1984, five Eddy kites rose to an altitude of 500m (1,640ft), carrying a series of instruments for measuring the air's temperature.

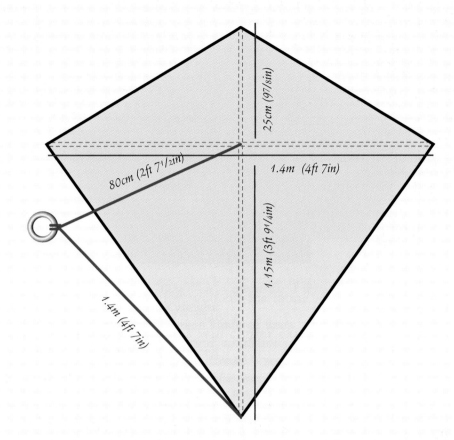

25cm (9⁷/₈in)

80cm (2ft 7¹/₂in)

1.4m (4ft 7in)

1.15m (3ft 9¹/₄in)

1.4m (4ft 7in)

The slight curve of the traverse makes the kite extremely stable. It also means that the kite can fly without a tail. The curve is made by stretching a line between the two ends of the traverse. The depth of the curve should be equal to about one tenth of the length of the kite.

12cm (4³/₄in)

Glue

There are various different kinds of glue – strong glue, glue for wood, cardboard, fabric or metal, glue in powder form which has to be diluted in cold water.

You can make your own glue at home. Mix 100g (3¹/₂oz) flour with 2l (70fl oz) water and bring it to the boil. Stir until the mixture is sticky. Use a brush to spread the glue on the surfaces you want to stick together. Heat the glue in a bain-marie the next time you want to use it.

Fish glue in flake or powder form makes the surface of the paper more solid.

This glue must be left to soak in water for an hour, then melted in a bain-marie, mixed with chalk and wood, and used hot. It should be spread in layers and left to dry.

Apart from glue, transparent adhesive tape can be used in kite construction. Wrapping tape or paper adhesive tape may also be used – and the latter can even be painted.

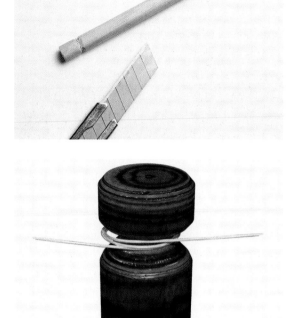

Making an Eddy kite

Take two rods. Use a cutter to make a 0.1cm (¹/₃₂in) notch around the ends of the rods.

Use a bowline knot to tie strong twine or fishing line to the end of a rod. The knot must be tightly tied inside the notch you have already made. Tighten the twine or fishing line so that the rod flexes like a bow.

Use a bowline knot to tie the line to the opposite end of the rod.

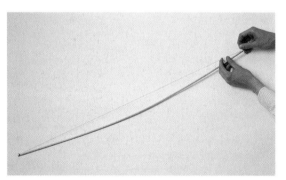

Make sure that the curve of the bow is regular and symmetrical.

Use a set square to make sure that the two rods are at right angles to each other.

Tie the two rods together with strong twine. Pull the line tight and use a double knot to tie it, then apply a drop of glue.

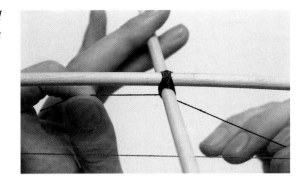

Tie one arm of the cross using a bowline knot and use the line to form the outline of the Lozenge or Diamond.

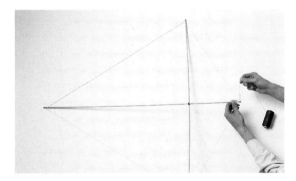

Use a set square to check that the two rods are still at right angles to each other.

Place the frame on a piece of paper and use a long ruler to trace the outline of the sail. Cut out the paper, leaving a margin of 1cm (3/8in) all around the edge of the kite.

If you are making a kite of more than one colour, stick the different-coloured pieces of paper together with glue. Make sure that this operation is carried out on a perfectly flat table.

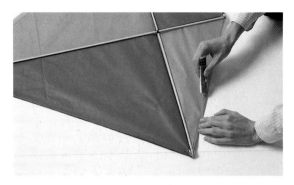

Proceed to the covering stage. Fold the cover over the framing line and fix it with glue.

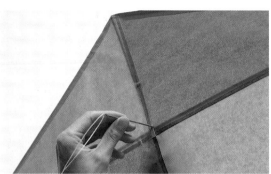

Attach the bridle to the kite. Use a large needle to make a hole in the covering at the point where the two rods cross. Attach the bridle to the frame at this point.

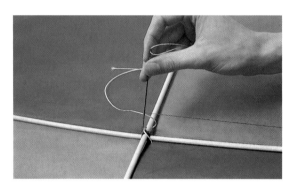

Use a cow hitch to make a ring on the fixed bridle – this will be the fastening point for the bridle line.

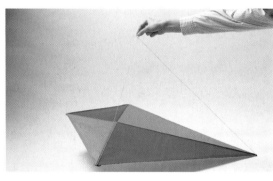

Knot the other end to the bottom of the kite. Find the correct arrangement by holding the kite above a flat surface. If necessary, loosen the hitch and move the ring until the kite is at an angle of about 15° from the flat surface.

Use your imagination to decorate the covering.

You can use indelible felt pens to decorate your kite. Be careful not to make any holes in the kite – proceed in small sections, using a light touch and taking care not to push the point of the pen through the covering.

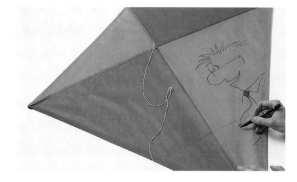

Do not use fabric or acrylic pens, as they will deform the paper and make the kite too heavy.

Your kite will need a tail in order to fly. Cut out a series of strips of paper about 3cm (1⅛in) wide and 20–25cm (7⅞–10in) long.

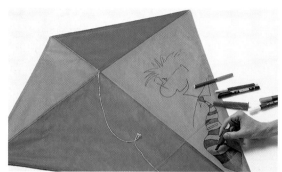

Make a chain by sticking the ends of the strips of paper together and threading them through each other to make a series of rings or links.

Fix the tail to the bottom end of the kite and then let your masterpiece take to the air!

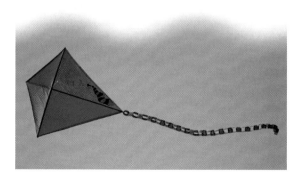

A kite train is a spectacular construction. Many different kinds of kites are used to make trains, but the most common are those that can be made fairly quickly – such as the Lozenge or Diamond, the Eddy or the Square.

Kite trains can reach high altitudes even when there is only a slight wind – as long as it is steady and if the bridle is regulated in the correct way, the train will continue to rise.

The first kite train was constructed in Scotland in 1749. It was made by Alexander Wilson, an astronomy professor, in order to measure the air temperature at different altitudes.

The record for the longest kite train is held by a Japanese flyer, who succeeded in flying 11,284 kites connected to each other by a single line.

I f you decide to construct a kite train, you should remember that the power of all the kites is added together, so the towline must be of the correct size.

Launching the train can be difficult, but the problem can be resolved by using a pilot kite. Attach it to the front of the train at a distance of about 8–10m (26–33ft) from the next kite. Use a kite of the same kind as the others, but of a larger size. If there are changeable wind conditions, use a stable flyer such as the Delta.

Some statistics

- *The greatest altitude reached by a single kite is 3,801m (12,467ft). The largest kite, which measured 750sq m (8,070sq ft), was first flown in Florida, USA, in 1995.*
- *The fastest kite reached a maximum speed of almost 193kph (120mph).*
- *The longest kite train was constructed in Japan in 1990. 11,284 kites took to the air, connected to each other by a single line.*
- *The longest flight for a kite took place in the USA in 1982. The kite remained in the air for 180 hours and 17 minutes.*

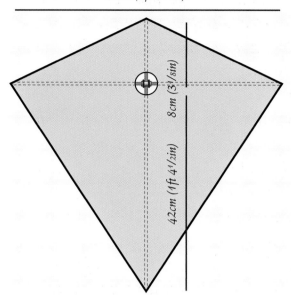

42cm (1ft 4¹/₂in)

8cm (3¹/₈in)

42cm (1ft 4¹/₂in)

1 **Sails** Cut out the sails from Tyvek or spinnaker nylon. Make the central hole as shown. Sew a hem around the kite. Make a pattern out of cardboard, as there will be many sails.

2 **Frame** Use one rattan rod of 21cm (8¹/₄in) and the other of 50cm (1ft 7⁵/₈in) with a diameter of 4mm (¹/₈in) and a V joint with a diameter of 4mm (¹/₈in). Connect the two traverses in the aluminium tube.

3 Fix the covering to the frame. Add three 4cm x 1.5m (1⁵/₈in x 5ft) tails.

15°

Insert a 0.1cm (¹/₃₂in) line through the hole in each kite and tie it to the frame. Leave a distance of about 30cm (1ft) between each kite. Use a line to attach the towline to the lower end of each kite. The first kite, the pilot kite, which should be larger than the others, must be about 15m (50ft) ahead of the rest.

Pilot kite

26cm (10¹/₄in)

41cm (1ft 4¹/₈in)

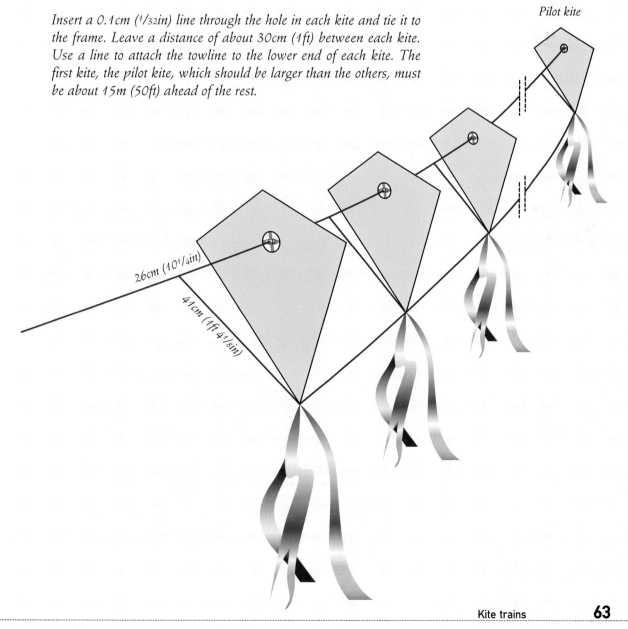

The Delta kite

Francis Rogallo started a real revolution with the research and experiments he carried out with regard to flying techniques.
His flyer, which was similar to a wing, led to the creation of the Delta kite, the Deltaplane and a kind of parachute for spaceships or jet pilots. The frame of the Delta is made up of a central longeron or spine, two laterals and a wingspan traverse.
The sails or covering are made of paper or fabric. The kite has a keel with three fastening points for the towline.
It is a very versatile kite. The ventral fin gives it stability, and the two wing longerons, which stop before meeting the central rod, mean that the kite's handler can adapt quickly to changes in the direction and strength of the wind.

The Delta flies by exploiting thermal air currents and in wind speeds from below 5 kph (3mph) to 45 kph (28mph). The ventral fin, with several fastening points for the towline, functions as a bridle.

You should always use good-quality lines that have a high level of tensile strength, so that they can withstand considerable tractive force.

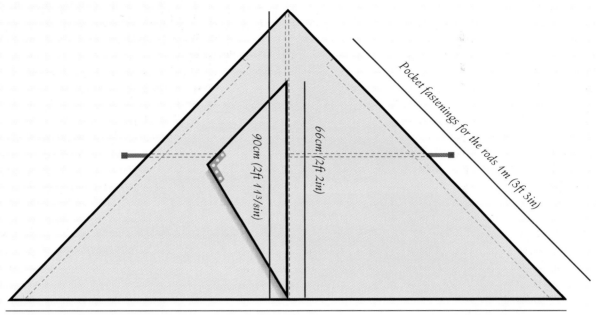

Pocket fastenings for the rods 1m (3ft 3in)

90cm (2ft 11³⁄₈in)

66cm (2ft 2in)

1.8m (5ft 11in)

The strength of the Delta means that it can raise tails and turbines of considerable dimensions. You should not, however, attach tails or turbines to the ends of the two wing longerons as this will bend the frame.

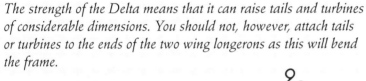

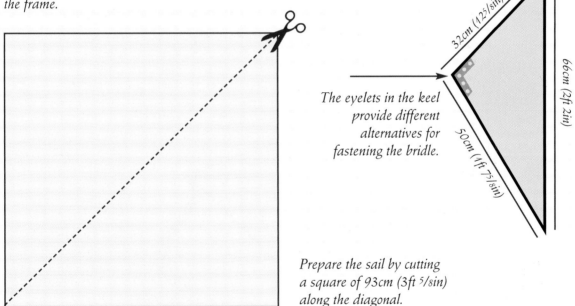

32cm (12⁵⁄₈in)

66cm (2ft 2in)

50cm (1ft 7⁵⁄₈in)

The eyelets in the keel provide different alternatives for fastening the bridle.

Prepare the sail by cutting a square of 93cm (3ft ⁵⁄₈in) along the diagonal.

MATERIALS

- Large triangular sail
- Ventral fin (the smaller triangle), which is sewn in the centre of the large sail
- A strip of Dacron or other strong nylon material, to strengthen the fastening point for the towline
- Three pieces of elastic for blocking the rods
- Two strips of spinnaker material
- Two tubes of perforated rubber for holding the central longeron or spine

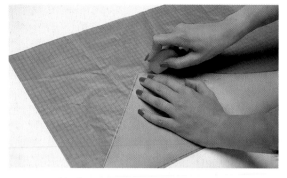

Making a Delta kite

Use wrapping paper to make a pattern, taking into account the margins for the seams, the hems and the pocket fastenings for the rods. Place the sections of the pattern onto the fabric and use sewing pins to fix them in place. Use tailor's chalk to draw the outline.

Remove the paper pattern and cut around the outline on the fabric. To make the hem, turn the fabric over, fix it with adhesive tape and sew. Remove the adhesive tape once the hem has been sewn.

Sew the hems and the pocket fastenings on the back of the kite. The front side must be perfectly smooth so that the air can pass over it without creating any disturbance.

Use a pair of scissors to cut sections of perforated rubber tubing – they should be 3cm (1¹/₈in) long. Use a punch to make holes in them 0.7cm (¹/₄in) from the edge. Insert the strip of spinnaker material, which should be folded in half, through the hole to make an eyelet.

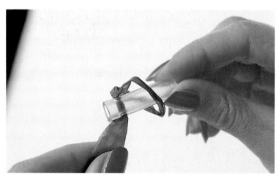

Pass the long side of the tube through the eyelet. Pull the two ends of the strip of spinnaker material so that the eyelet adheres to the tube.

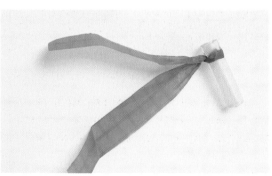

Now the fastening for the longeron or spine is ready to be sewn.

To make the kite stronger, use a sewing machine to sew a double hem along the ventral fin. Double-sew the thread at the beginning and end of each seam and secure it well. When you hem the corners, do not cut the thread – rather, make a single seam.

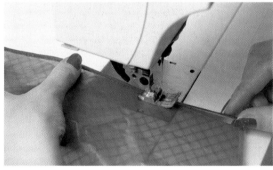

Sew a double strip of Dacron onto the longer side. This will strengthen the kite at the point where the towline is fastened.

When Mother Carey's chickens (otherwise known as storm petrels) fly towards the sea, it means that a storm is coming. In fact, these sea birds have no problem with stormy seas – the wind disturbing the waves makes it easier for them to catch fish.

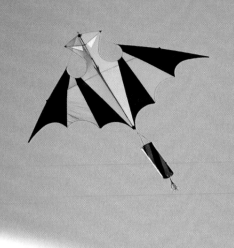

Even fleas can predict the weather.
When they bite a lot at night, it means that the weather
is going to change!

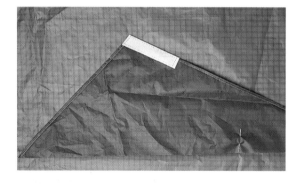

Use a hot, sharp piece of metal, such as a skewer, to make holes in the Dacron at regular intervals.

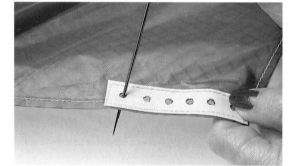

Push the piece of metal through the hole several times to make sure that the hole is a regular shape. The heat will melt the fabric and make it secure. Sew the hem on the largest sail.

Take into account the diameter of the rod which has to be inserted and then sew a second seam to make the pocket fastening.

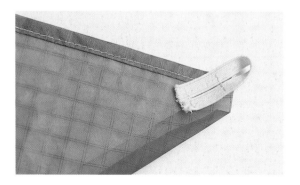

Position a piece of elastic folded in half. This will keep the rods steady inside the pocket fastening and will make it easier to replace the rods if they should break. Sew a seam along the four sides.

Fold the spinnaker material and prepare the pocket fastening for the rod on the other side. Sew a piece of elastic – which will fix the central longeron or spine – onto the centre of the large sail.

Place the ventral fin on the centre of the material and fix it in place with sewing pins. Fold the material along the line where the ventral fin meets it, and sew a seam along the centre.

Turn the material at the pointed end of the kite and close the pocket fastening with two overlapping seams.

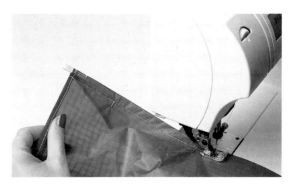

The strips of Dacron connected to the rubber tubes should be sewn onto the two wing longerons, on the right side up and folded towards the back. Insert the longerons into the tubes.

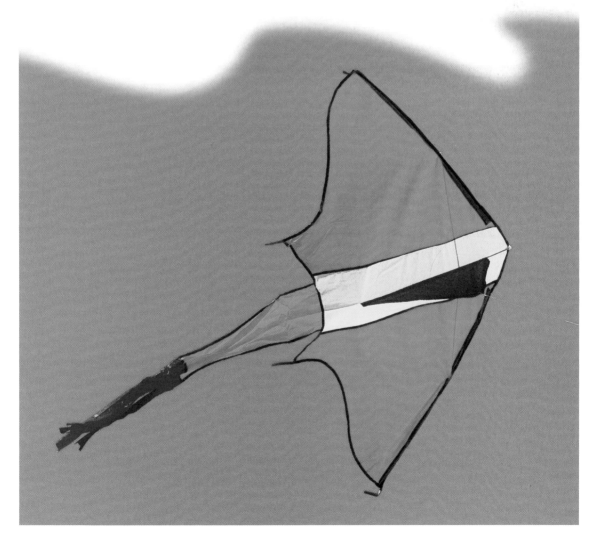

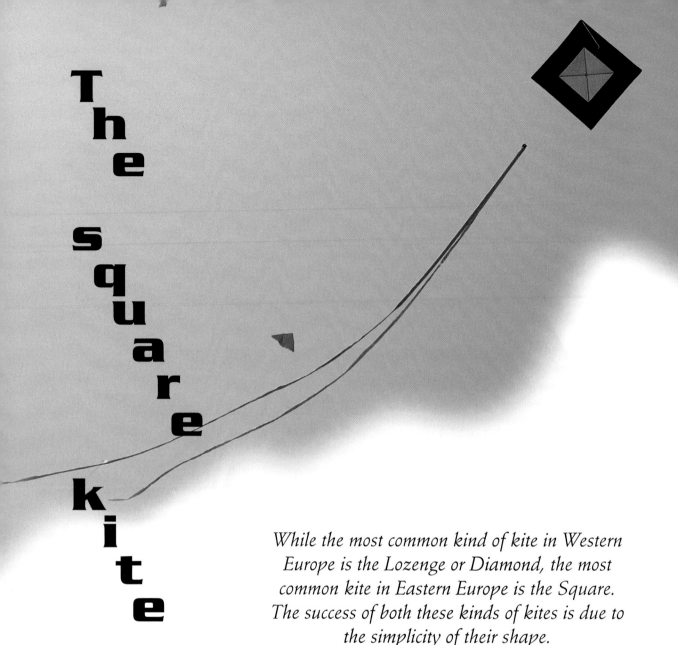

The Square kite

While the most common kind of kite in Western Europe is the Lozenge or Diamond, the most common kite in Eastern Europe is the Square. The success of both these kinds of kites is due to the simplicity of their shape.

The large surface area of the sails and the light weight of these kites make them ideal flyers in moderate wind conditions. They can, however, spin around in stronger winds or during gusts or squalls. These kites can be of any size – just make sure that the rods are strong enough to bear the weight of the kite.

Although these kites have a very simple shape, it is essential when making them to check that the frame and the sails or covering are completely symmetrical, and that the bridle is of the correct size.

The three-line bridle is attached to the front ends of the diagonals, and at the point where the splints cross.

The tail should be about 10m (33ft) long, and should be attached to the bottom ends of the splints.

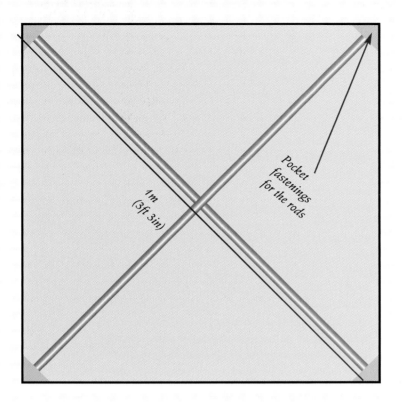

1m
(3ft 3in)

Pocket
fastenings
for the rods

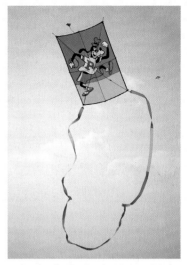

A rectangular kite based on the Square kite. The tail is attached to the bottom corners of the kite.

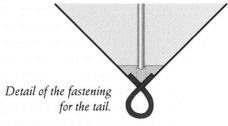

Detail of the fastening for the tail.

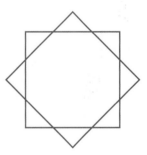

An interesting variation on the Square kite, using two squares one on top of the other.

A Square kite is made of two rods that cross each other, and a sail. Like the Lozenge or Diamond kite – and flat or plane surface kites in general – this kind of kite needs a tail, which should be regulated at the flying site, after the wind conditions have been verified.

The square kite can stay aloft in a very light wind (5kph/3mph) and can fly well in moderate winds (20–28kph/ 12–17mph). Rods made of carbon fibre should be used, to make sure that the frame stays rigid during flight.

When launching a Square kite, it is best to use a high-start launch so that the kite leaves the area of ground turbulence as soon as possible.

Only fly this kind of kite at high altitudes if you are certain of good atmospheric conditions. Strong or changeable winds can cause the kite to fall to the ground.

Some people like to attach a line to the upper side of the kite so that it makes a buzzing sound when it comes into contact with the wind.

When fish leap out of the water again and again, it means that rain is on its way. When a storm is coming, flies look for the warmest areas on the surface of the water and the fish take advantage of this – like many other creatures, they eat a lot more than usual before a rainstorm.

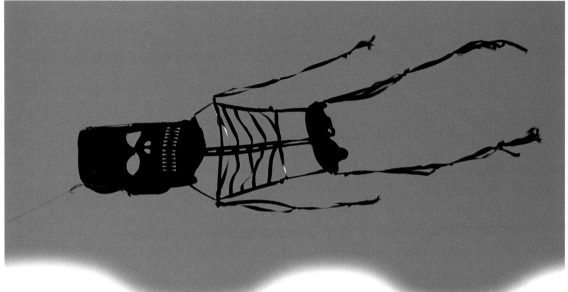

Sled kites

This kind of kite can be made of nylon, light plastic-coated canvas – or even a big rubbish bag. The Sled does not have any wingspan traverses or spars, so it is not rigid and it takes its shape from the wind.

This flying skeleton is made of a Sled (the head) and a woven tail for the body.

While the Sled is not the best flyer, it is an enjoyable kind of kite. As there are no traverses or spars to keep the covering open, the Sled has a tendency to collapse and fall to the ground during strong winds or rapid manoeuvres.

You can use polythene (plastic shopping bags) for the covering. The ideal place for flying this kind of kite is the beach, where a constant wind carries it to high altitudes in a short time.

The two lines of the bridle should be exactly the same length to ensure optimum flight, and each one should be twice as long as the kite itself. The kite must be launched as quickly as possible with a line that is not too taut, so that the kite does not turn back on itself. On the other hand, the line should not be too slack, either – in this case the kite will go limp. When you have acquired some experience, you will be able to fly the Sled in a stable fashion at a very low height – even just above your head. The Sled flies well in constant winds of 5–35kph (3–22mph).

Fishing with kites

The kite gave rise to the aeroplane and many other inventions. It has been used in signalling and observation missions and even for going fishing.

Fix a ring to the fastening point of the bridle or to a point on the towline. Attach a fishing line with a hook on it to the ring. Launch the kite. When it has stabilized, release the fishing line so that the hook enters the water.

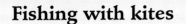

An owl made of coloured paper on a bamboo frame.

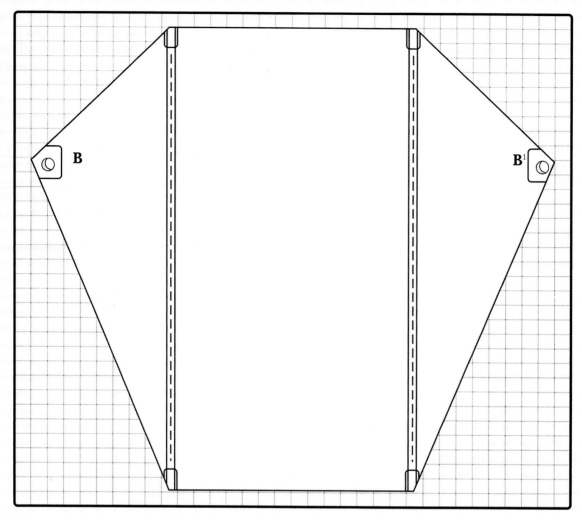

One square in the diagram shown above is equal to 5cm (2in).

Cut out the sails as shown in the diagram.

Prepare two passing holes for the rods.

Sew strips of Velcro around the edges of the passing holes.

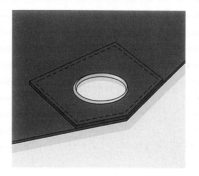

Use adhesive tape or Dacron to reinforce the fastening points for the bridle (B–B¹) and insert a metal ring.

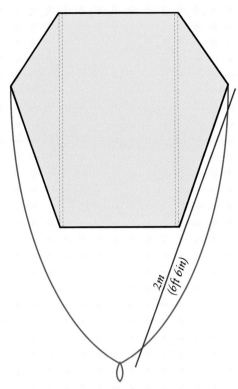

Fasten the bridle line at the points shown in the diagram. There should be a distance of 2m (6ft 6in) from the surface of the kite to the knot.

2m (6ft 6in)

A variation on a Sled kite. The two longerons have been replaced with pockets, which inflate in the wind.

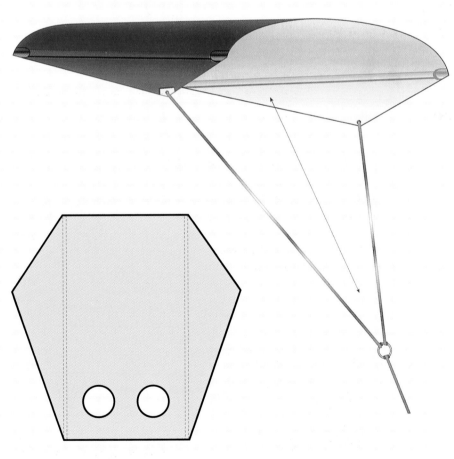

Make holes in the sails as shown in the above diagram – this will improve flying stability.

The Sanjo Rokkaku kite

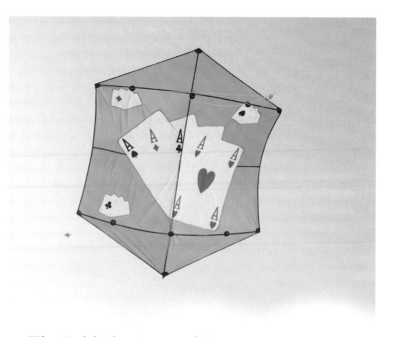

The Rokkaku is one of the greatest Japanese fighting kites. Sanjo is the name of a town, and Rokkaku means 'hexagon'. The name is pronounced with the accent on the final syllable.

This kind of kite is an excellent flyer in constant winds. It is strong enough to lift turbines, flags and various kinds of tails.

Construct your Rokkaku as you would a flat or plane surface kite, then curve the two traverses or spars. The curve removes tension from the sails or covering and has a stabilizing function – just like in the Eddy kite.

When flying this kind of kite, make sure that you check the tension of the towline constantly. It should always be taut. Only a slight wind (6–11kph/4–7mph) is necessary to launch the Rokkaku, but it can fly well in winds of up to 35kph (22mph). Use a very strong towline, and wear gloves if the wind is strong.

The enormous kites used for fighting are of a rectangular shape with a bamboo frame that is reinforced with diagonal rods. These kites can be up to 10m (33ft) wide and 15m (50ft) high and can weigh hundreds of kilograms. The diameter of the reinforcing rods is equal of that of a man's wrist.

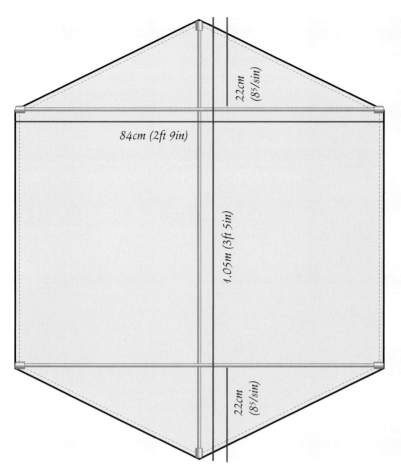

22cm (8⁵/8in)

84cm (2ft 9in)

1.05m (3ft 5in)

22cm (8⁵/8in)

Sew the pocket fastenings for the rods onto the sails, along with the reinforcements, including those for the lines.

The curve of the two wingspan traverses optimizes the stability of the keel when the kite is in flight. The diagram below illustrates the bow shape of the two transverse longerons.

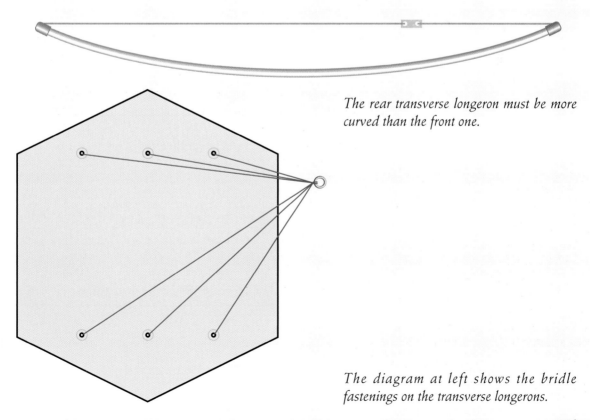

The rear transverse longeron must be more curved than the front one.

The diagram at left shows the bridle fastenings on the transverse longerons.

Assembling a Rokkaku kite

Sanjo Rokkaku kites have been used in Japan for more than three centuries to fight for honour and glory. The fighting teams are expert at controlling their kites.

The aim of the competition is to cut the towline of the opposing team's kite, or to use strategic moves to force it to the ground.

In the second half of the 19th century, an engineer of English origin called Lawrence Hargrave built the first cellular kite – the Hargrave Box kite. The Cube is one of the simplest of these kites to make.

L awrence Hargrave was born in Greenwich, London, in 1850, and emigrated to New South Wales, Australia, in 1866. The Cube is one of the kites that belongs to the large family of cellular or Box kites, the first of which was invented by Hargrave in 1893.

Hargrave separated the bearing structures of the kite from its stabilizing structures, creating a remarkably stable kite that was suitable for flying in strong winds – although not suitable for lighter winds.

A stiff breeze of 12–19kph (7–12mph) is essential for launching this kind of kite, while it should not be flown in winds of more than 50–60kph (30–40mph).

The sails or covering of the Cube should be kept taut, as is the case with all Box kites.

If the kite is bridled as shown on page 80, each surface will be provided with both a bearing and stabilizing function. The flying arrangement can be varied by using a four-line bridle, which will allow the Cube to fly with one side parallel to the ground. The two horizontal surfaces provide the bearing function; the vertical surfaces provide the stabilizing function.

The cube kite

The frame is made of two perpendicularly crossed traverses. Four longerons, perpendicular to the plane formed by the traverses, are placed at the ends of this structure as shown. They support the sails or covering.

The frame is made of round sections of rattan. The sails or covering are made of spinnaker fabric.

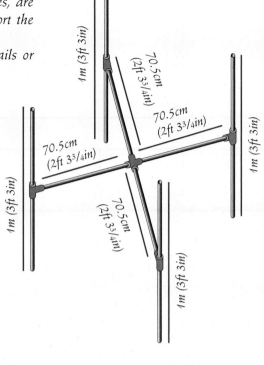

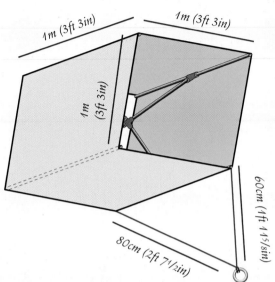

A two-line bridle is usually used.
If a four-line bridle is used, the kite will fly with one side parallel to the ground.

The Hargrave Box Kite

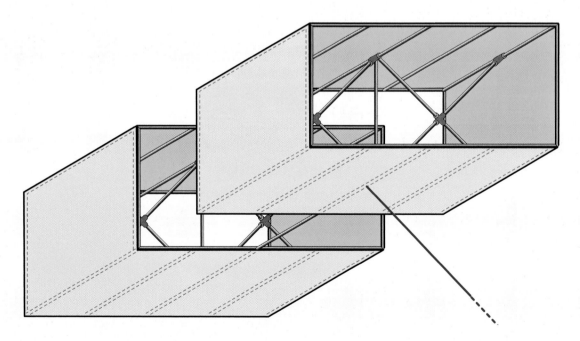

Hargrave's invention encapsulated all the aerodynamic discoveries of his time. His kites were used by meteorological observation stations in Europe. Box kites also made man-lifting safer – flat or plane surface kites had previously been used for this activity.

The Conyne kite

The Conyne is a Box kite with two very large wings. It is named after its inventor, an American called Silas J. Conyne, who patented his design in 1902. The Conyne kite is often confused with a similar kite which was invented by the Frenchman Louis Blériot in the same year. Blériot's kite was stronger, rigid and shorter in length, while the Conyne has non-rigid triangular cells and can be dismantled.

The Conyne kite has good flying qualities and can be transported easily – it can simply be folded up once the wingspan traverse has been removed.

In fact, the Conyne differs from other Box kites in that its cells become rigid according to the thrust of the wind. It flies well in wind speeds of 7–40kph (4–25mph).

The rods used for the frame are made of carbon fibre or rattan. You should use spinnaker fabric or lightweight paper to make the sails or covering.

The Conyne can be quite difficult to launch – a high-start launch is best to make it easier.

If you want to make your Conyne more stable, add a V joint at the central point of the wingspan traverse.

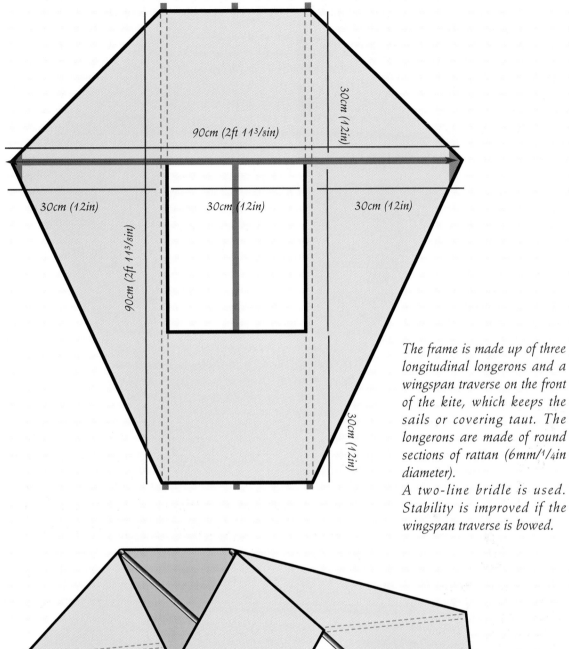

90cm (2ft 11³⁄₈in)

30cm (12in)

30cm (12in)

30cm (12in)

30cm (12in)

30cm (12in)

90cm (2ft 11³⁄₈in)

30cm (12in)

The frame is made up of three longitudinal longerons and a wingspan traverse on the front of the kite, which keeps the sails or covering taut. The longerons are made of round sections of rattan (6mm/¹⁄₄in diameter).
A two-line bridle is used. Stability is improved if the wingspan traverse is bowed.

1.6m (5ft 3in)

1.8m (6ft)

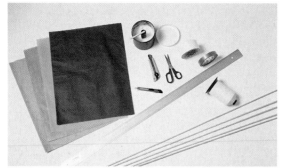

Making a Conyne kite

You will need tissue paper, rattan rods, scissors, a cutter, glue, a ruler, twisted nylon line and adhesive tape.

Join two 50 x 70cm (1ft 7¹/₂in x 2ft 3¹/₂in) pieces of tissue paper together to obtain a sheet of 100 x 70cm (3ft 3³/₈in x 2ft 3¹/₂in) as shown pink.

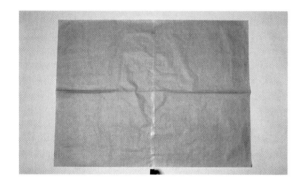

Mark the outline of the wing (length 90cm/2ft 11³/₈in, height 30cm/11³/₄in) and cut out the two pieces.

Join two 50 x 70cm (1ft 7¹/₂in x 2ft 3¹/₂in) pieces of tissue paper together to obtain a sheet of 100 x 70cm (3ft 3in x 2ft 3¹/₂in) as shown green.

If you want to know at what height your kite is flying, make a piece of equipment to give you the angle of flight.

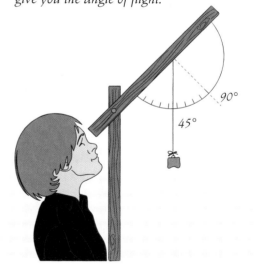

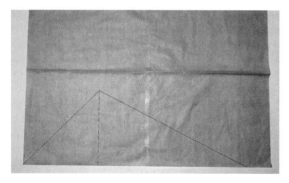

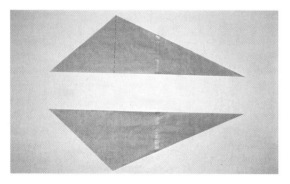

Cut out two 95 x 30cm (3ft 1³/₈in x 11³/₄in) rectangles from the sheet of green paper.

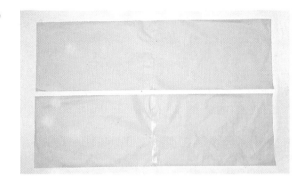

Place the pieces as shown in the diagram, making sure that you keep to the divisions of 30, 30 and 30cm (11³/₄, 11³/₄ and 11³/₄in).

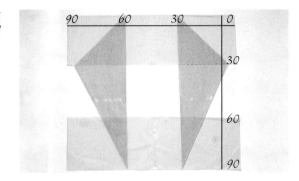

How to calculate the height of your kite

There are many methods based on the properties of similar triangles. While one person holds the line, the other stands directly under the kite. A third person holds a set square at eye level and observes the kite until it can be seen on the extension of the set square. To calculate the height of the kite, multiply the distances AB–AD and divide the result by the distance AE. The quotient gives the height at which the kite is flying.

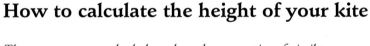

Join the wings to the rectangles that form the cells.

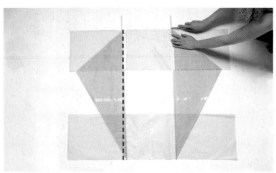

Cut the two vertical rods, place them on the covering and fix them.

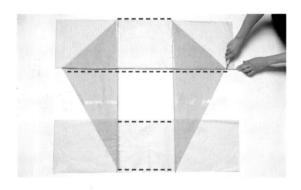

Cut the 90cm (2ft 11³/₈in) rods and fix them to the covering. Join the short sides of each rectangle, making sure that you keep to the divisions of 30, 30 and 30cm (11³/₄, 11³/₄ and 11³/₄in).

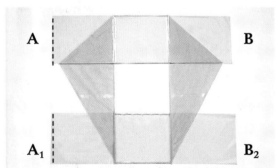

Join the sides as follows: A with B and A_1 with B_2.

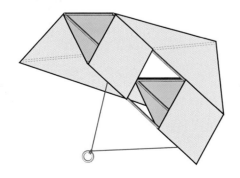

Fix a 90cm (2ft 11³/₈in) rod inside and at the centre of the two trihedrons.

Attach the two ends of the bridle line.

This kite is based on a design
by Stephen Robinson.
Its shape is similar to a snowflake,
from which it derives its name.

This kite has good lifting qualities in light winds, due to its lightness and large sail area.

As the Snowflake is three-dimensional in construction and has a rigid frame, several of these kites can be joined together by connecting the sides of the hexagonal edges. In this case, the tops of the kites should also be connected to each other to make the overall structure more manageable.

The Snowflake kite

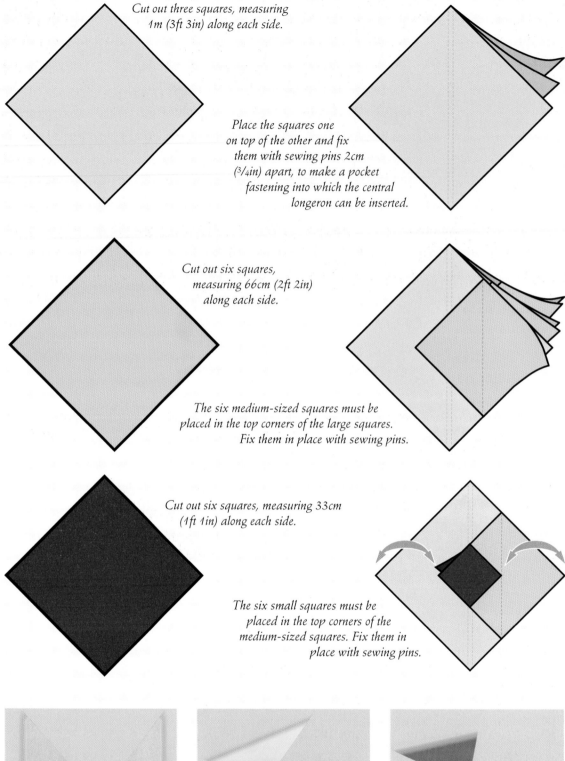

Cut out three squares, measuring
1m (3ft 3in) along each side.

Place the squares one
on top of the other and fix
them with sewing pins 2cm
(³/₄in) apart, to make a pocket
fastening into which the central
longeron can be inserted.

Cut out six squares,
measuring 66cm (2ft 2in)
along each side.

The six medium-sized squares must be
placed in the top corners of the large squares.
Fix them in place with sewing pins.

Cut out six squares, measuring 33cm
(1ft 1in) along each side.

The six small squares must be
placed in the top corners of the
medium-sized squares. Fix them in
place with sewing pins.

Join the tops of the squares together
with strips of spinnaker nylon.
Attach a ring for each strip.

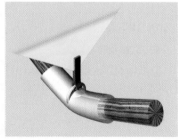

Use pieces of tubing for the
connections.

Pass the rod (the edge of the kite)
through the rings.

To make the frame, you will need seven rods of 1.5m (4ft 11in) length, 50cm (1ft 7⁵/₈in) of plastic tubing with a diameter of 0.8cm (⁵/₁₆in) and some nylon line.

Use spinnaker fabric for the sails or covering. Make the longerons from sections of rounded rattan with a diameter of 1cm (³/₈in). The most difficult phase is sewing the seams – try to be very precise.

When you have finished making the covering, connect the six rods that form the edge of the kite, and then the central longeron.

Because it has so many vertical surfaces, the Snowflake remains very stable in changeable wind conditions.

If you join several of these kites together, remember to calculate their overall tractive force.

This kind of kite can fly in a light breeze (about 8kph/5mph) or a stiff breeze (38kph/24mph).

If the wind is medium or variable, you should use a very strong towline. The Snowflake modifies its tractive force in variable wind conditions, even if the changes in wind speed are very slight.

Cut out the sails against the weave of the fabric. Make sure that you leave enough spare fabric (1–1.5 cm/³/₈–⁵/₈in) to sew double hems.

Use spinnaker fabric for the sails or covering. Carbon fibre can also be used for the rods.

Box kites in the sky and at the flying site.

The illustration on the right shows how the various parts of the Snowflake kite look when they have been sewn together. The largest sails are shown here in blue, the medium ones in orange, and the smallest ones in pale green.

A variation on the Snowflake kite, designed by Stephen Robinson.

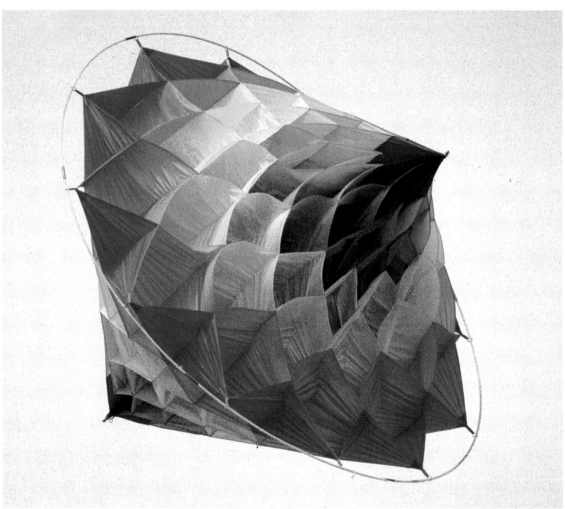

The Bell's Tetrahedral kite

The tetrahedral kite is made up of equilateral triangles with an internal angle of 60°. Each kite is a module that can be assembled together with other modules.

Spinnaker fabric is used for the sails or covering. The frame is made of fibreglass or wood (diameter 6mm/¼in). The joints can be made of aluminium tubing. The bridle is two-line.

Figurative kites

Because bamboo is so flexible, it has been used with great success in the construction of figurative kites by master kite-makers in the Orient. They are able to shape the bamboo with great expertise and then make fantastic coverings for their kites in fabric or paper.

Before beginning to work with bamboo, it is a good idea to spray it with insecticide to make sure that it does not get eaten away by parasites – which will obviously cause it to split or break.

Flatten the internal parts with a file or hammer. Use steam or a flame to heat the bamboo when you want to bend it. Handle it with care to avoid getting splinters in your hands.

Many kites are designed to imitate exactly the animals or people that they depict – butterflies, dragonflies, beetles, cicadas, bees, eagles, hummingbirds, seagulls, hawks, ducks, penguins, tortoises, fish, samurai, warriors…

Pigs can fly!

The head of a peacock.

Centipede kites

Centipede kites originated in China. They are fascinating to watch, as they imitate the creature they depict in their movements, as well as in their colours and shapes.

There are two kinds of centipede kites. In China, the body of the kite is made with circles of decreasing size, while in Japan circles of the same diameter are used.

In the Orient, it is usual to build centipede kites of 80m (260ft) in length, made up of 160 circles. There have even been stories about kites of 130m (425ft) in length, made up of 260 circles.

In the West, centipede kites are generally about 20m (65ft) in length and are made up of 40 circles.

This kind of kite is easy to build, but a lot of patience is required. The most difficult operation is bridling the circles, which make up the body, in such a way that each one of them is perfectly parallel to the next one. The centipede is probably the most difficult kite to launch, but once it is in the air it undulates steadily.

A centipede kite small enough to fit into a matchbox…

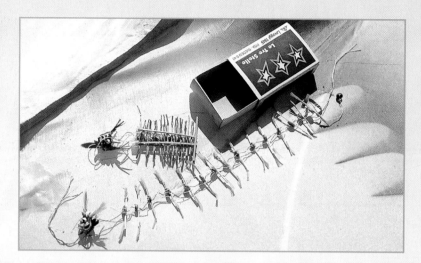

… but it can still fly.

A steady, stiff breeze is necessary for launching a centipede kite. Place the circles one on top of the other on the flying site, while a helper holds the first circle (the head). The first circle will pull all the others and the kite will move gracefully into the sky.

The centipede kite is made up of rings covered in coloured paper and connected to each other in a line. The rings can be made of cane.

Make a circle with a diameter of 40cm (1ft 3³/₄in).

The traverse rods are made of bamboo.
Fix strips of paper, feathers or streamers to the ends.

The circles should be 30cm (12in) apart and must be connected to each other by three lines.

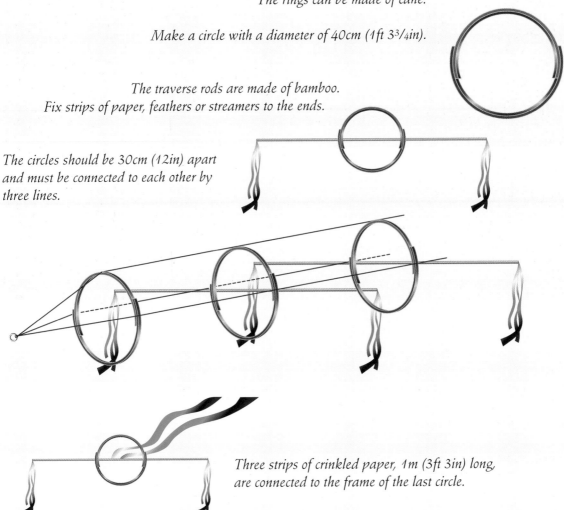

Three strips of crinkled paper, 1m (3ft 3in) long, are connected to the frame of the last circle.

A crocodile's head – all set to lead a fantastic centipede kite into the air.

The Circoflex kite

Designed by Helmut Schiefer and Ton Oostveen, a Circoflex 750 is a kite made of polyethylene and 0.3cm (1/8in) fibreglass. It is suitable for flying in light winds.

The experiments go on and on... the Hargrave Box kite, the Bell's Tetrahedral kite, Rogallo's Delta, Domina Jalbert's Parafoil, the Flexifoil, the Peter Powell kite and stunt kites, Peter Waldron's Prof, Martin Lester's Shark and Crane, New Zealander Peter Lynn's dragonfly...

Going to kite festivals is a good way of seeing the latest models and finding out how to build them – you can get all the details from the experts themselves.

The Seagull kite

Richard Bach's Jonathan Livingstone Seagull *is not like other seagulls, who think eating is more important than flying. He preferred to fly. He wanted to find freedom in the sky.*

The Seagull kite is based on the Delta kite, and can fly at high altitudes. Although it has a very light frame and a reduced sail surface, these factors are not detrimental to its flying qualities.

This kite is not suitable for lifting windsocks or tails. It rises very rapidly and has a very wide attack angle, so any change in the tension of the towline or in the direction of the wind means that the wings of the kite will fluctuate. In fact, its graceful shape is designed to emulate the beating of a seagull's wings.

This kite will fly in a light breeze (6–11kph/4–7mph) or a stiff wind (29–38kph/18–24mph).

It is necessary to pay particular attention to the fastenings of the towline in order to achieve the correct flying configuration. Attach the line to the hole in the head of the Seagull in the case of a stiff wind, or move the fastening towards the tail if the wind is lighter.

Use a lightweight line with a low break strength for the towline. In fact, this kind of kite does not exert a lot of tractive force.

The Seagull is a variation on the Delta kite.

Draw the shape of the bird on the covering and take great care in cutting it out. Make sure that you leave a border wide enough for hemming and reinforcing the fabric and for avoiding any tearing.
Fringe the lower part of the fabric to simulate the wings of the bird, as shown. Trim the pocket fastenings for the wing longerons and sew them with care.

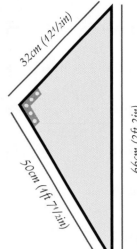

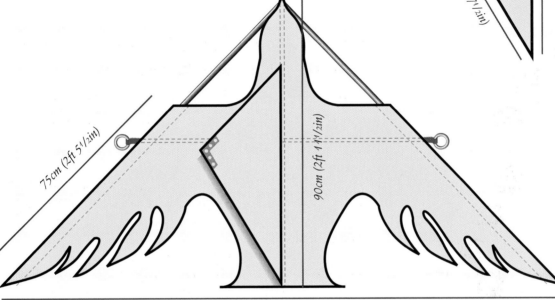

1.8m (6ft)

A lot of information can be found on the Internet about kites... historical information, photographs, dates of meetings and festivals, instructions on steering and controlling stunt kites, diagrams, stories, legends, fables, poetry... and specialist kite shops. Listed below are just a few of the many sites:

www.kites.org	*A general, non-commercial kite site*
www.kiteconnection.com	*A general kite site*
www.tako.gr.jp	*Japanese kites*
www.revkites.com	*Revolution kites*
www.kites.tug.com/law	*Kite-flying competition rules*

Sailing Ship kites

The man behind this fantastic kind of kite is Medio Calderoni – a real artist as far as kites are concerned. His workshop in Ravenna, Italy, has been the theatre for the creation of kites in the shape of sailing ships, birds, butterflies, Viking longships and various different characters.

Medio Calderoni is capable of incredible inventiveness and artistry when he is faced with an aerodynamic problem relating to a Sailing Ship kite.

He has won international renown as an expert in the art of kite-making, and has taken part in numerous kite conventions throughout Europe.

Some of Medio Calderoni's most fantastic creations are his flying Sailing Ships. It is quite difficult to describe how to build them, but the following diagrams illustrate the main steps. Anyone who wants to make one of these kites has to face the problems that arise in constructing it with practical know-how and creativity.

You will need to find some canes, which can easily be found near streams and rivers. They must be fairly thick, strong and solid. You should cut them into sections and, according to how thick they are, bend them over a flame (see page 23).

The diagram below shows how to connect the various rods, using thread and glue. Let the glue dry before proceeding to the next step.

The Hull

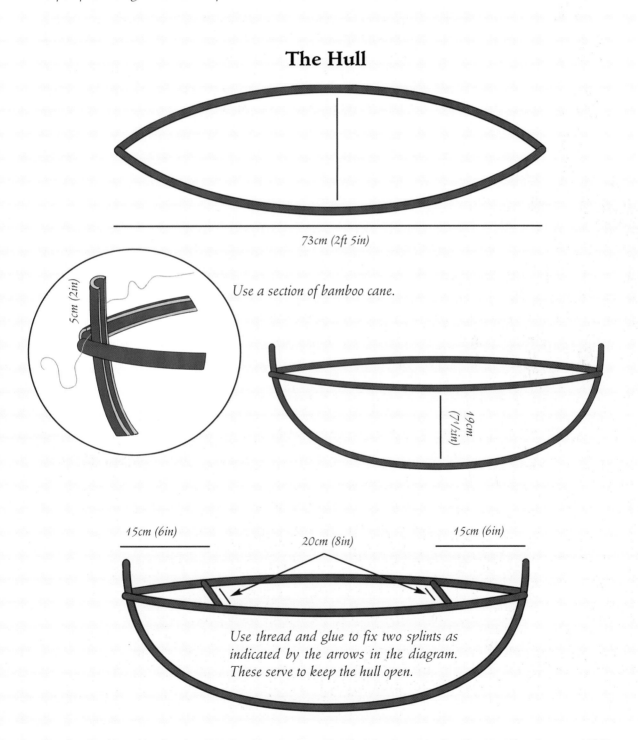

73cm (2ft 5in)

Use a section of bamboo cane.

5cm (2in)

19cm (7½in)

15cm (6in)   20cm (8in)   15cm (6in)

Use thread and glue to fix two splints as indicated by the arrows in the diagram. These serve to keep the hull open.

The masts

Use an entire cane for the mast and a section for the traverse rods, as indicated in the diagram below. Add other splints to strengthen the frame.

Front　　　　　　　　　　**Back**

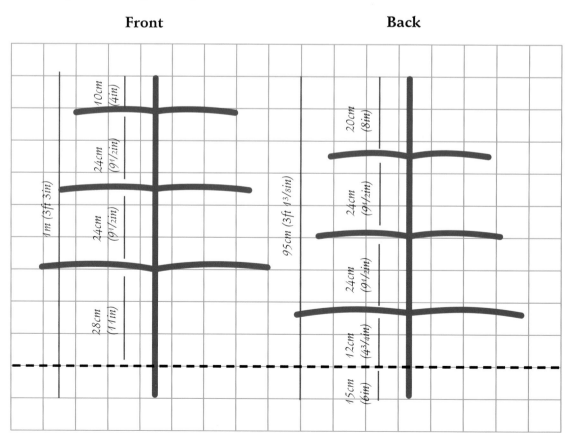

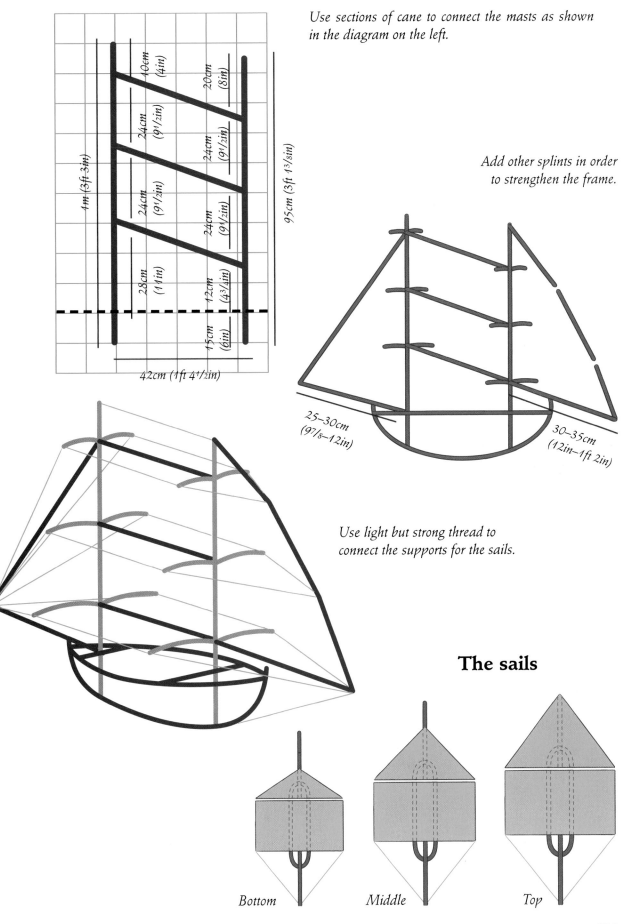

Use sections of cane to connect the masts as shown in the diagram on the left.

Add other splints in order to strengthen the frame.

40cm (4in)

20cm (8in)

24cm (9¹/2in)

24cm (9¹/2in)

24cm (9¹/2in)

24cm (9¹/2in)

4m (3ft 3in)

95cm (3ft 1³/8in)

28cm (11in)

12cm (4³/4in)

15cm (6in)

42cm (1ft 4¹/2in)

25–30cm (97/8–12in)

30–35cm (12in–1ft 2in)

Use light but strong thread to connect the supports for the sails.

The sails

Bottom

Middle

Top

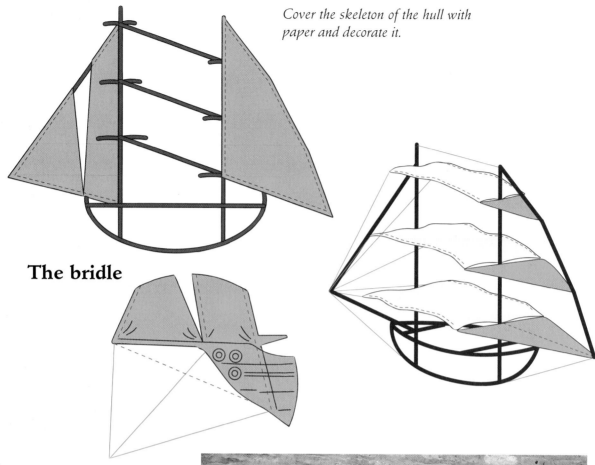

Cover the skeleton of the hull with paper and decorate it.

The bridle

Connect the bridle to the front part of the Sailing Ship as shown.

The Nagasaki Hata kite

The Nagasaki Hata is a fighting kite. Rice glue mixed with powdered glass is attached to the towline, near the kite itself. During fighting contests, the kite's handler tries to cut the line of the opposing kite, so that it falls to the ground. It is a tradition in the Orient that a fighting kite that is defeated becomes the property of the person who picks it up.

The frame of the kite is made of splints of wood (traditionally, sections of bamboo) or fibreglass. The sails or covering are made of spinnaker fabric, kite paper (parchment) or silk.

This kind of kite has a two-line bridle – each line is twice the length of the kite. It is necessary to be very careful when selecting the point at which to attach the bridle line: the attack angle must be lower than that which is normally used in other kites. It should be between 5° and 10°.

Twisted nylon line should be used for the towline.

The Nagasaki Hata flies in light to medium winds. It flies in a stable manner only when the towline is taut. If it should slacken, the wingspan traverse returns to an upright position and a curved kite becomes a flat one. This instability can be exploited by the handler to perform significant manoeuvres.

The bridle lines should be regulated in accordance with the wind conditions.

The Hata's traditional colours are red, white and blue.

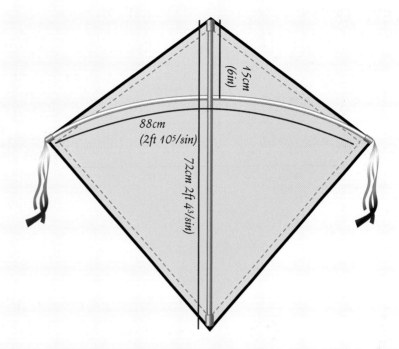

Every year in Japan, many kite competitions are held between March and May. They are big festivals, and the battles between kites are carried out in a sporting spirit.

The name Nagasaki Hata comes from the city of Nagasaki and the Japanese word 'hata', which means 'flag'. This kite flies very fast and responds quickly.

Great precision is necessary when making a Hata. Symmetry is a crucial factor: the wingspan traverse must flex symmetrically when the kite is in flight. To ensure that this happens, you must taper the longitudinal longeron and the wingspan traverse with great care, in order to make sure that the points where the kite receives the pressure to perform its manoeuvres are very sensitive and are able to respond quickly.

Do not change the measurements of the design shown here. Fighting kites must be built strictly in proportion in order to ensure maximum speed.

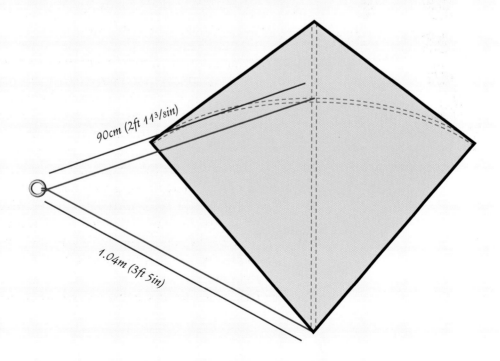

It is quite difficult to launch a fighting kite, but kite-flying philosophy in Japan holds that no aid is allowed. The kite's handler must rely on expertise and, at most, the help of a young assistant, whose only role is to stow any excess line in a basket and make sure that it does not become tangled or knotted.

Steering a fighting kite

The principle that governs flying a fighting kite is based on the flexion of the wingspan longeron and, thus, on changes in the dihedral angle.

If the towline is not taut, the kite will lose stability and become a flat, or plane surface, kite. It will vibrate in the sky and turn around on its own axis.

As soon as the handler tightens the line, the kite responds by flexing the wingspan longeron and changing into a bowed kite with the correct configuration – which is provided by a positive dihedral wing. The kite will then fly as straight as an arrow, following the direction of the point at its peak.

You can perform all sorts of stunts with a fighting kite. You can bring it to within a few metres of the ground and then make it swerve and rise into the sky again. In order to do this, slacken the towline when the kite is still high in the sky – it will begin to rotate.

When the point of the kite is aimed at the ground, tighten the line again by pulling your hand in towards your chest. The kite will plunge sharply. When it is within a few metres of the ground, slacken the line again. If the kite is well made, it will respond immediately by stopping, rotating on itself with precision and then turning its point upwards. If you tighten the line again, you will see your kite rising swiftly into the sky.

During competitions, all manoeuvres must be carried out at great speed, so the towline is left on the ground. The movements of the kite are controlled by pulling the line to the right or to the left in such a way as to adjust the point at which lift is applied. When the line is slack, the kite will begin to swing and it will seem that it is about to fall to the ground. Tighten the towline to make it rise again.

A fighting kite in the sky has to cut the line of its opponent's kite. When this happens, the kite's handler shouts 'Katsuro!' The crowd runs towards the defeated kite, and the first person to reach it and pick it up becomes its new owner.

The fighting kite originated in India. It was probably introduced into Japan by Dutch merchants – who were the only merchants allowed into the port of Nagasaki – about halfway through the 16th century.

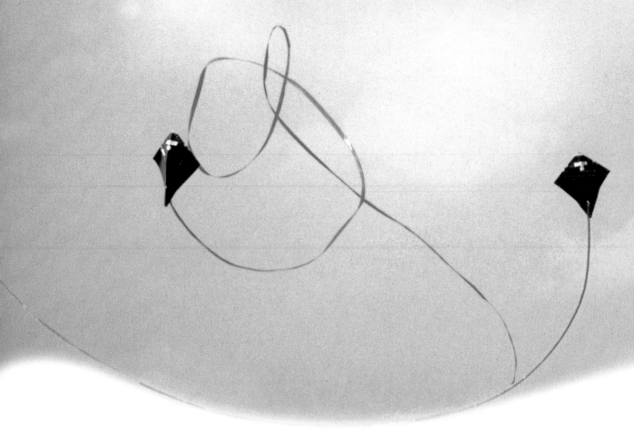

The Peter Powell kite

How will your kite fly if you fasten the towline to two sections of the bridle, one of which is longer than the other? Your kite will fly in the direction of the shorter line, and will begin to turn around on itself. Now imagine that you have two towlines, each of which is attached to two sections of the bridle. If you pull each line in the same direction, using the same amount of pressure, your kite will fly in a straight line. But if you pull the two lines in different directions, using a different amount of pressure, the kite will perform a series of acrobatic stunts. This is the principle behind the stunt kite.

The Peter Powell kite falls into the category of two-line stunt kites. It is controlled by means of two handles, which vary the tension of the two towlines. The resulting imbalance to the left or right determines the way the kite moves in the air. After some practice, it is possible to carry out loops, swoops and other complex manoeuvres.

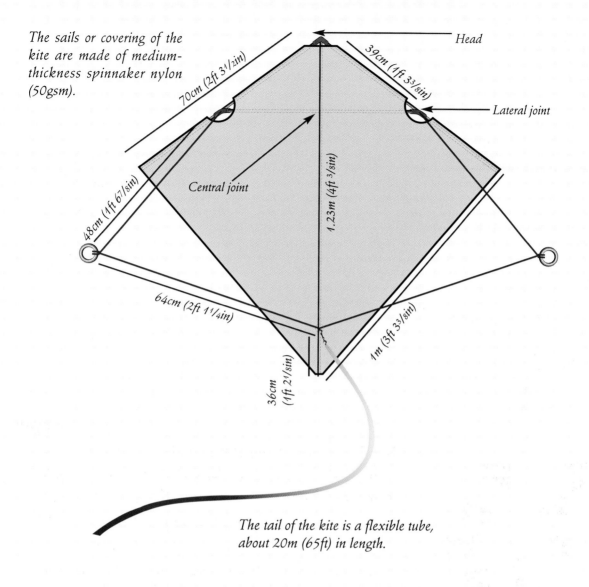

The sails or covering of the kite are made of medium-thickness spinnaker nylon (50gsm).

Head

70cm (2ft 3½in)

39cm (1ft 3⅜in)

Lateral joint

48cm (1ft 6⅞in)

Central joint

1.23m (4ft ⅜in)

64cm (2ft 1¼in)

1m (3ft 3⅜in)

36cm (1ft 2⅛in)

The tail of the kite is a flexible tube, about 20m (65ft) in length.

The joints are made of rubber tubes, into which fibreglass rods are inserted.

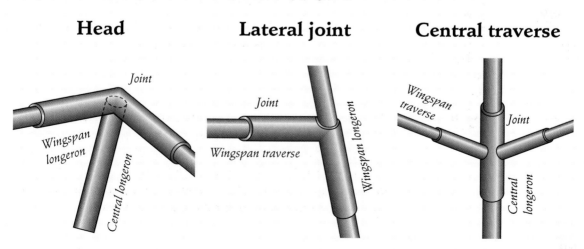

Head

Joint

Wingspan longeron

Central longeron

Lateral joint

Joint

Wingspan traverse

Wingspan longeron

Central traverse

Wingspan traverse

Joint

Central longeron

Swift stunt kites.

The Peter Powell is an ideal kite for anyone who wants to try stunt flying. This type of kite flies at an easily controllable speed and is extremely robust – a useful factor if it should fall to the ground. It can fly in medium winds, but it moves with amazing speed in strong winds.

The lines must be strong and should be replaced frequently because constant friction during flight means that they wear out rapidly.

Fly this kind of kite at an altitude of 25–30m (80–100ft). Do not launch it in crowded areas, and make sure that no one is standing within its range. If you lose control, the kite will dive towards the ground at a speed of more than 100kph (62mph), therefore turning itself into a highly dangerous weapon.

During the 1970s, there was renewed interest in traditional kites, although in modified form. The Diamond kite, for example, gave rise to a new generation of fast kites. An English kite maker called Peter Powell designed a kite that was highly manoeuvrable and fast and which could perform amazing stunts. This kind of kite is easy to assemble, even when making a kite train. Its tubular tail, about 20m (65ft) long, creates a wonderful impression as it follows the kite in the air.

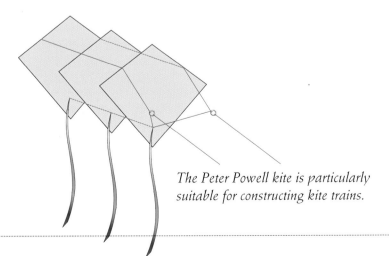

The Peter Powell kite is particularly suitable for constructing kite trains.

You need a lot of space and a little wind to make your stunt kite perform incredible feats. There are three kinds of stunt kites – single-line, double-line and quad-line.

Double-line stunt kites

Double-line stunt kites are steered with two handles or a handlebar about 1–1.2m (3–4ft) long, to the ends of which the towlines are attached.

Launching Place the kite 30m (100ft) away from you. Pull the two lines at the same time. The kite rises with the thrust of the wind and performs like a static flyer, with a single central bridle and a single towline.

Flying When you change the tension of one of the two lines, the kite swerves to the right or left and performs a series of amazing turns. Do not go too far, as if the lines slide over each other the kite does not respond well to your commands. The high level of friction can lead to dangerous wear and tear, which ultimately results in one or both of the lines breaking.

Do not perform more than four or five turns in one direction before making the same number of turns in the other direction, so that the lines return to their original parallel position. After a little practice, you will be able to skim the kite just above the ground, or make it dive to the ground and use the point of a wing to tear away tufts of grass.

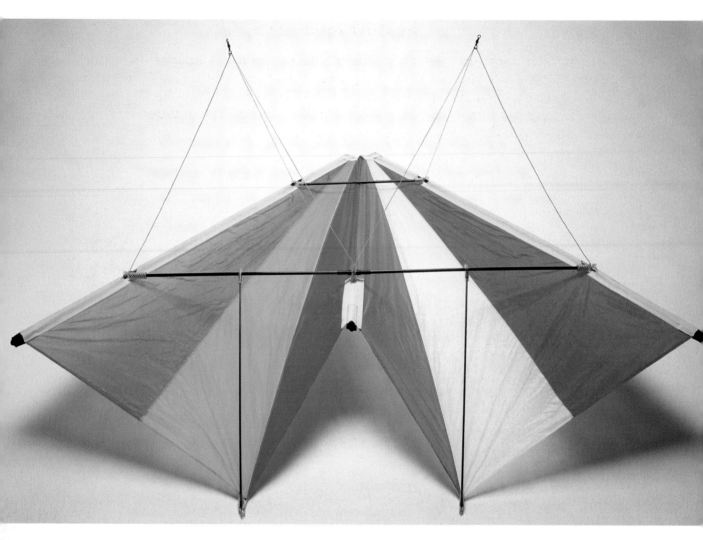

A modern, fast double-line stunt kite.

Quad-line stunt kites

There are not many quad-line stunt kites, but the best-known is the Revolution.

This kite can move in a similar way to a helicopter. The handler uses two handles to control the flight. Each handle has two lines.

The handles are alternately moved towards and away from the handler's body. If the handler rotates his or her wrists so that the handles are at an angle, the kite's attack angle to the wind can be varied.

There are a combination of main movements that mean that the kite can turn around on itself, land on each of its sides, take off in any position and stop a few centimetres from the ground and hover above it.

The imagination of kite flyers and the potential of stunt kites have lead to many impressive, creative stunts. Someone has even tried fixing a paintbrush to the frame of a stunt kite and painting a picture with it.

The Revolution kite

The Revolution is a modern stunt kite controlled by means of four lines. It can move like a helicopter, stopping a few metres above the ground. It can turn around on itself and perform all kinds of stunts. Many high-precision competitions are organized for these kites – the people taking part have to make their kites insert one of their tips into a glass on the sand, for example, or make them fly through a narrow passage.

A Revolution ready to take off.

When the two handles are pulled with equal force, the kite will rise into the sky, ready to perform a series of amazing stunts.

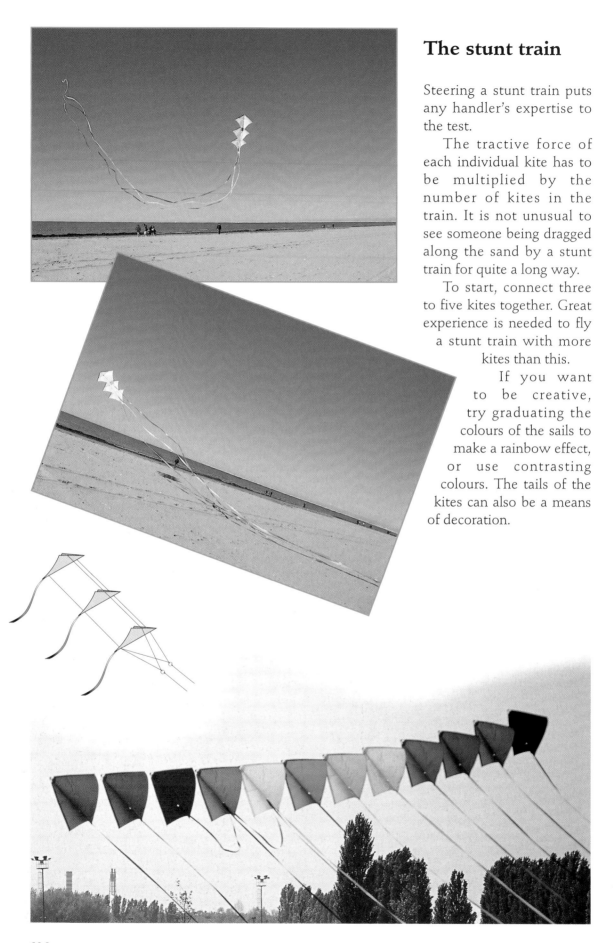

The stunt train

Steering a stunt train puts any handler's expertise to the test.

The tractive force of each individual kite has to be multiplied by the number of kites in the train. It is not unusual to see someone being dragged along the sand by a stunt train for quite a long way.

To start, connect three to five kites together. Great experience is needed to fly a stunt train with more kites than this.

If you want to be creative, try graduating the colours of the sails to make a rainbow effect, or use contrasting colours. The tails of the kites can also be a means of decoration.

Kites
in Flight

Why do kites fly?

Kites are aerodynes.
This means that they exploit the aerodynamic
action of the wind in order to fly.

The way a kite flies is determined by changes in the strength and direction of the wind, by the movement of its sails and by the flexibility of its frame.

Complex physical laws combine to keep a kite in the air. It is much more difficult to explain *how* they fly than it is to actually fly a kite.

The towline, which anchors the kite, creates a resisting force which combats the force of the wind, and thus makes the air push against the lower side of the kite in such a way as to support it.

The tail also provides resistance and stability according to its type, its length, its weight and – above all – the distance from its fastening point.

Winged kites

There are many winged kites, such as Parafoils or Flexifoils, which exploit the hydrodynamic principle formulated by Bernoulli (see over), which states that the pressure exercised on a surface by a fluid is inversely proportional to the rate at which it flows.

Daniel Bernoulli
(1700–82) was a Swiss scientist who formulated the basic principles of hydrodynamics. The laws of physics mean that an increase in the speed of the flow of a fluid over a surface (such as the wings of aeroplanes or propellers of ships) corresponds to a decrease in the pressure exerted on the surface itself.

The flight of an object is determined by its weight, its resistance to the wind and by the supporting aerodynamic action.

Weight *Kites are subject to the laws of gravity. Weight can be represented on a graph with a downward vertical arrow (the vector) that begins at the barycentre of the kite.*

Wind resistance *Unlike weight, wind resistance is a horizontal force that goes against the direction of the wind. It can be illustrated by drawing a horizontal vector at the point of the barycentre.*

*The sum of weight and resistance together result in a downward vector with an angle of between about 40° and 60°. In order to fly in a balanced fashion, a kite must develop an opposing force of equal intensity to that of the wind and an opposing direction (**supporting aerodynamic action**).*

The air flows over the upper and lower surfaces of a wing at a different speed, and so exerts a different level of pressure.

Winged kites have a great lifting capacity. Stability is provided by vertical keels. This kind of kite can fly close to the ground.

In 1963 Domina Jalbert designed the Parafoil – a winged kite made entirely of fabric. The Parafoil takes its shape from the wind as it passes through the openings between the kite's surfaces, which are connected by bands of fabric. Although the two surfaces are not always parallel, they form the shape of a wing.

All the bridle lines are connected to a series of ventral keels and are then linked to a single towline. This means that the kite is very stable.

Banners at a flying site.

Flying sites

The best flying sites are large open fields or beaches.

Y̶ou need to understand how to spot the best kinds of flying sites if you want to get the best from your kite.

A hill site has many advantages. Launch your kite about 30m (100ft) from the top of the hill, on the side exposed to the wind. The kite has time to overcome any ground turbulence, and you can go up to the top of the hill and enjoy the breeze.

Your kite will not fly if you try to launch it from the side opposite the wind.

Look for a wide open space without any obstacles – like a deserted beach…

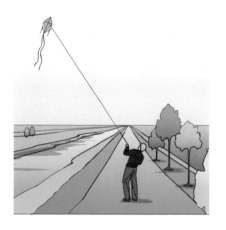

a big meadow…

You should always be ready for little emergencies. Make sure you always carry nails, quick-drying glue, spare rods, adhesive tape, paper or other material for the sails or covering, a pair of scissors and spare tails.

or near a river. The best kind of site slopes slightly in the same direction as the wind.

Kites can get into trouble! You can be sure that if you are near a tree, your kite will get tangled up in it. Why does this happen? Because trees create eddies of air around them, which will attract your kite.

When you carry your kite, hold it by the frame, not by the sails or covering.

Do not run like a mad thing to launch your kite – you will just make all the expert kite-flyers laugh! In Kensington Gardens, London, there is a hill with a little house on top. Behind the house are benches where elderly gentlemen sit, calmly launching their kites and watching them fly in the air.

Where not to fly your kite ...

*between houses and
television aerials...*

*Near high-voltage electricity
lines or pylons...*

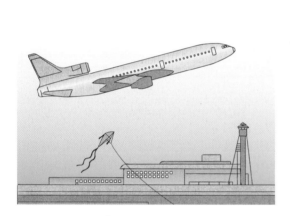

near sea ports or airports...

on crowded beaches...

during a storm...

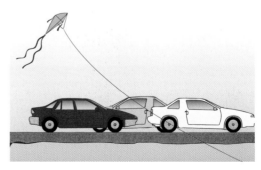

or near roads or motorways.

*While you do not need
a pilot's licence to fly a kite, it is just as well
to follow some rules.*

When you fly your kite, pay great attention to how it behaves. Try to remember what kind of tail you are using and how long it is, what kind of towline you have attached, and how fast the wind is. All this will help you avoid repeating any mistakes the next time you go out to fly your kite.

Taking off

If your kite is well made and there is enough wind, it should take off without any problem when you throw it up into the air.

If there is not enough wind, you will have to look for it at a higher altitude. This means trying a high-start launch. Kites will usually fly in winds of 5–30kph (3–19mph).

Turn your back to the wind and unwind a few metres of line. Pull slightly and the kite will rise. Let the line play out evenly and not too quickly, so that the kite can gain height.

The right kind of wind

A stiff, steady wind is the best kind for flying kites.

Although you can fly kites at any time of the year, the best season is the spring.

Do not make the mistake of trying to fly a kite that is not suitable for the kind of wind conditions you are facing. It is, for example, a bad idea to keep on trying to launch a Box kite if there is not enough wind. You should take different kinds of kites with you, to cover a range of wind conditions.

WIND STRENGTH	0	1
Metres/feet per second	0–0.2/ 7½ in	0.3–1.5/ 8in–5ft
kph/mph	<1/<1	1–5/1–3
Description	*Calm, smoke rises vertically.*	*Wind direction just shown by smoke, not by weathervanes.*

Flying

When flying your kite, check the tension of the towline. If the kite begins to drop due to lack of wind, rewind the line quickly. On the other hand, if the kite becomes unstable due to a gust of wind, stabilize it by playing out more line. Obviously, the steadier the wind, the easier it will be to fly your kite.

Continue to play the line in and out so that the kite can gain altitude, and remember that the higher the kite flies, the less quickly it will respond to commands via the towline.

Sometimes, a kite begins to fly parallel to the wind. This means that it flaps like a flag and begins to drop towards the ground. If this happens, you should give the line a sharp tug in order to return your kite to the correct position.

The Beaufort scale

In 1805, an Admiral in the British Navy called Sir Francis Beaufort formulated a table that showed a wind velocity scale. This meant that it was possible to estimate the speed of the wind. The threshold value, after which it is dangerous for small boats to take to the sea, is Force 6. Do not try flying your kite if the wind is any stronger than this, as you will risk losing it.

2	3	4	5	6
1.6–3.3/ 5ft–10ft 8in	3.4-5.4/10ft 9in–17ft 9in	5.5-7.9/17ft 10in–25ft 11in	8.0-10.7/ 26–35ft	10.8-13.8/ 35–45ft
6–11/4–7	12–19/8–12	20–28/13–18	29–38/19–24	39–49/25–30
Wind felt on face; leaves rustle.	*Leaves and small twigs in motion.*	*Dust rises; small branches move.*	*Small trees in leaf begin to sway.*	*Large branches move.*

The high-start launch

This is a technique for launching your kite in a large open space.

Ask a friend to stand a considerable distance away from you, holding the kite.

When you give the signal, your friend should let the kite go – but should not throw it!

You should run back from where you were standing for a few metres, and the kite will gain height.

If there is still not enough wind as the kite gains height, play out the line. The kite will fall and move further away. When the kite is a few metres from the ground, rewind some of the line quickly and the kite will start to rise again – it will reach a higher altitude that the previous one. Repeat this procedure.

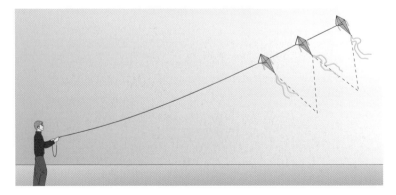

Landing your kite

In medium, steady winds your kite should return to you easily. Do not try to bring it down too fast, and be patient if there are gusts of wind. The critical landing phase is when your kite is about 30m (100ft) from the ground.

If the wind is very strong, send the kite to an altitude of about 30m (100ft). Then give the winding reel to someone else and walk towards your kite, letting the line run through your hand – which should be protected by a glove and at least one handkerchief. The kite should return directly to your hand.

Problem solving

Here is some advice to help you solve some of the problems that can arise during launching, flying and landing your kite.

The basic rule for a trouble-free flight is to try, try and try again until you find ideal wind conditions.

The kite rises with difficulty.

It is probably too heavy in relation to the strength of the wind, or maybe the attack angle is wrong. Reduce the length of the tail and

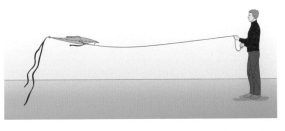

adjust the fastening point of the towline to the bridle. Move it forward if the front part of the kite rises too sharply. Move it back if the kite flies flat and beats the air.

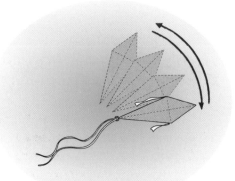

The kite pitches and swerves, *and the tail whips in the wind. Lengthen the tail and move the bridle ring forwards.*

The kite turns around the line, *like a dog chasing its own tail. Slacken the line. In many cases, the kite will then assume the correct configuration on its own. If this does not happen, bring the kite down. Maybe the tail is too short, the shape of the kite is asymmetrical so that the weight of the kite is unevenly distributed, or the tension of the bridle is uneven. You should lengthen the tail, make sure that the various parts of the kite are balanced in relation to each other, and check the length of the bridles.*

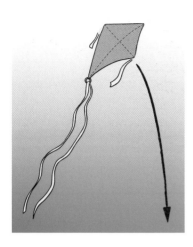

The kite goes into a nose dive. *In this case, the bridle is too long. Move the fastening point closer to the sails or covering. Increase the size – and therefore the weight – of the tail.*

The towline droops. *Wind it in a little, as it is too heavy for the kite.*

The kite pulls on the towline too much. *Let the line go a little and then bring the kite down, or hook windsocks or turbines to the towline.*

Mistral

A cold, dry wind which blows from the north west. It is said to bring good weather, and is particularly common in the southern Mediterranean area.

Windsocks

Windsocks are tapered cones that turn around on themselves. They are made of colourful triangles of fabric, which create an attractive decorative effect in the sky. Windsocks, like tails, can provide kites with greater stability.

A windsock is a particular kind of tail that moves in the sky by turning around on itself. The wind is the 'motor' that makes the windsock turn. It causes a rotating movement in the windsock when it enters the windsock via pockets in its structure.

If the windsock is made of strips of different coloured fabric, it creates a kind of colourful spiral effect as it turns around and around. It is possible to make windsocks that rotate at different speeds – you just have to vary the number of triangles that make up the windsock, as well as the shape and width of the pockets. So, you can create different effects – if your windsock is big and rotates slowly, it will seem heavy and ponderous; if it is long and thin, it will appear nimble and agile.

You can use a windsock to decorate the towline, or as a stabilizing tail. Its gyroscopic effect will provide your kite with greater stability.

The windsock shown in this chapter can be adapted to suit many different kinds of kites.

Making a windsock

You need spinnaker nylon, a polyvinyl chloride (PVC) tube, a cylindrical wooden rod (to be inserted into the tube), nylon line and a snap hook reel.

Cut out three 1.5m x 10cm (5ft x 4in) rectangles along the diagonal from the nylon, so that you have six triangles.

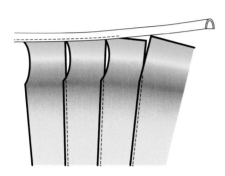

Sew the six triangles together – but do not sew the first 10cm (4in) or the last 40cm (1ft 4in), so that they are staggered from each other at a distance of about 3cm (1¼in).

Next, join the first and sixth parts together.

Cut out a 62 x 5 cm (2ft ³/8in x 2in) strip of nylon. Fold the larger side in half and sew it so that it forms a pocket. Sew the hem of the pocket along the bottom of the six triangles.

Insert the polyvinyl (PVC) tube into the pocket and use a piece of the cylindrical rod to connect the beginning to the end.

Attach four lines to the tube, using a snap hook reel.

If you want to make an effective kind of weathervane, attach a wind turbine to the end of a fishing rod. Push the rod vertically into the ground at the flying site. Then observe the direction of the turbine in order to discover the direction of the wind. The rotation speed will provide you with an anemometer, which will give you a good idea of the speed of the wind.

Rotors with a horizontal axis

Kite festivals are a kind of theatre, displaying a wide range of flying objects. Weathervanes, soap bubbles, spirals… they all play in the wind.

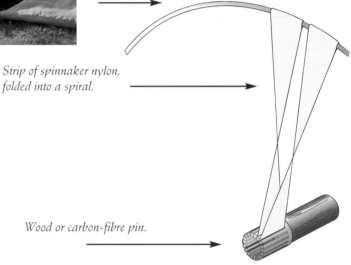

Fibreglass circle, diameter 3–4 mm (¹/₈–⁹/₆₄in)

Strip of spinnaker nylon, folded into a spiral.

Wood or carbon-fibre pin.

Rotors with horizontal axes, designed by Heinz Tlotzeck.

In the Orient, people used to fly musical kites above their houses at night to keep away evil spirits.
In fact, the Chinese name for a kite means 'aeolian harp', which is a harp that is played by the wind.
If you want to bring the night to light, you can attach a series of lights to the line of your kite, or fasten little battery torches to its frame.

Musical kites

It is said that Huan Then, a Chinese general who was also a scientist and an advisor to the Emperor, once saved the Chinese people from a barbarian invasion during the time of the Han dynasty (200BC–200AD).

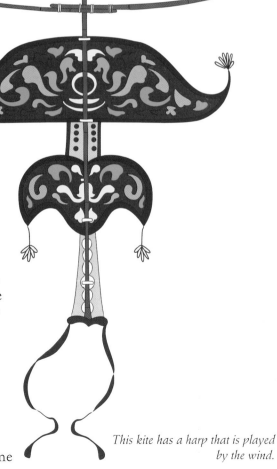

The Imperial Palace was under threat from the enemy forces. Huan Then was ordered to organize the defence. He climbed up to the highest part of the Palace to assess the situation.

Suddenly, his hat was blown away by a gust of wind. As he retrieved it and replaced it on his head, he had an idea.

He ordered that a great number of kites be made. Each one carried a wind harp – a bow stretched by a very thin line. The kites were launched at dead of night. The wind carried them towards the enemy camp, and the sounds that they made frightened the enemy soldiers to death. They took to their horses and fled in disarray.

It is still a tradition in the Orient to fly musical kites above houses at night to keep evil away.

In Malaysia, Kelantan kites are frequently fitted with a bow that makes music. According to tradition, the kites come

This kite has a harp that is played by the wind.

Here are two ways of fixing a guitar string to an Eddy kite. The taut string makes sure that the traverse of the kite is kept tight.

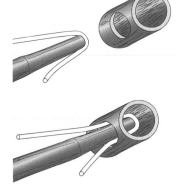

alive as soon as they sound the first note when they take to the air.

In Japan, children attach more than one harp to their kites, so that they create a kind of orchestra in the skies.

A taut towline will also create vibrations. A famous example of this took place at Cervia, Italy, when a song by Lucio Dalla was played on a kite during a kite festival.

You can make your kite sing by fastening strips of paper along its longerons.

Use a guitar string to curve the rod of an Eddy kite (see page 56). This will produce a sweet sound. If you use two guitar strings, you will make even better music!

If you are flying a big kite, you can even attach a flute to the frame, but take care to keep an even balance.

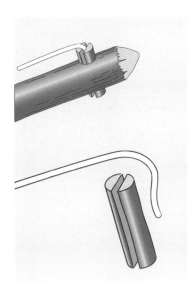

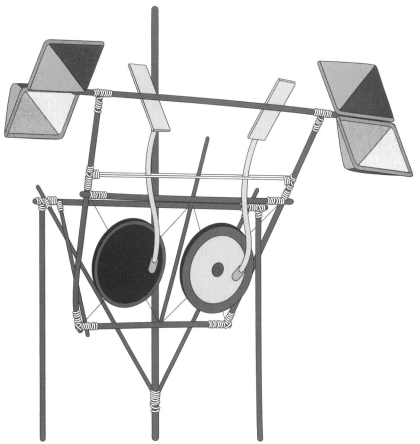

The configuration of a musical kite. The rods push the hammers to beat the drums, due to the action of the wind.

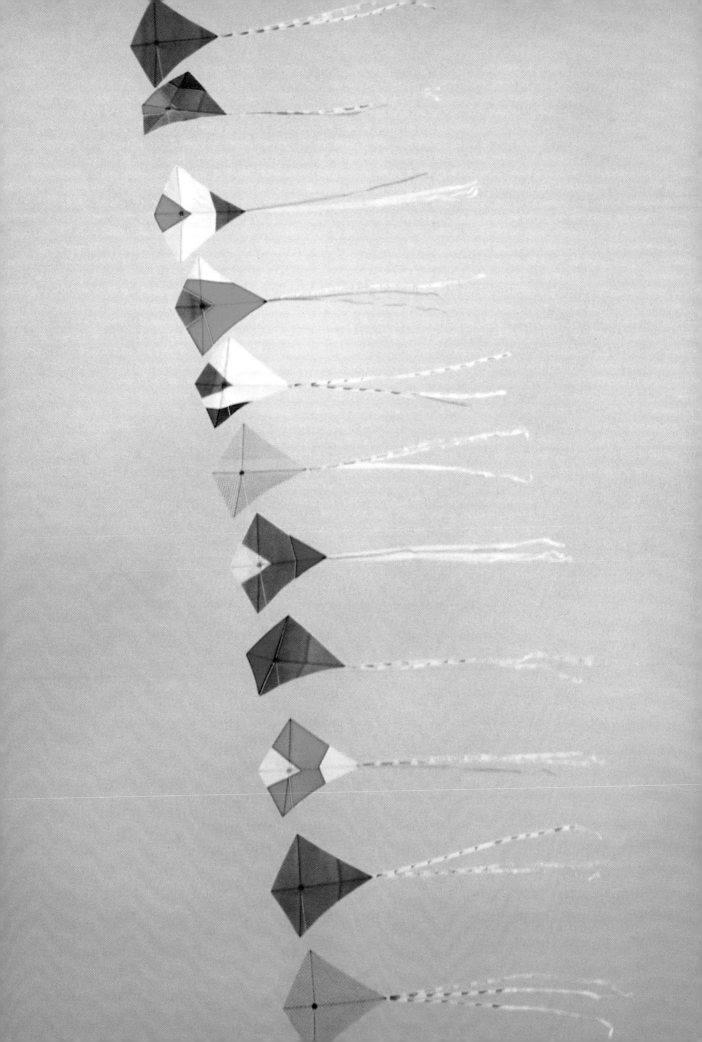

Southwester

This wind blows from the south-west. It is called 'Garbino' or 'Africo' along the Adriatic coast. It is unpredictable, and frequently brings rain.

Kites with lights

You can light up your kite when it is flying, creating a wonderful effect. Connect pocket torches to it, but make sure that everything is well-balanced and symmetrical. You could even outline your kite in lights and use coloured ones for even greater effect.

You can arrange small lights on a transparent or semi-transparent covering, so that they form a design. You can also fix a row of lights to your kite's tail, making sure that they are secure.

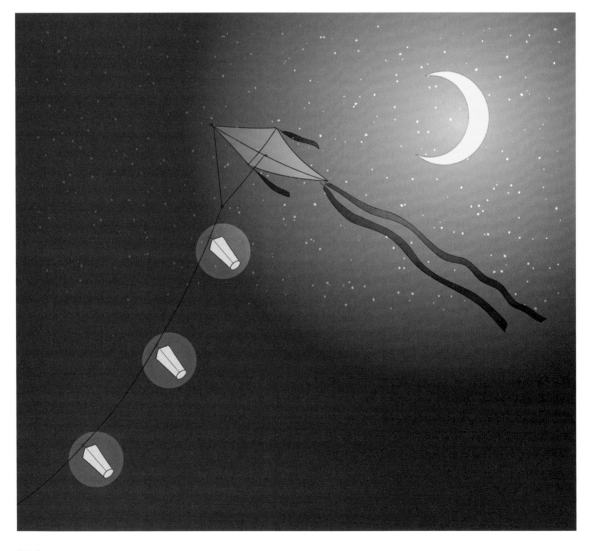

Flambeaux

Attach light holders to the towline of your kite to create a magical atmosphere in the night sky.

Connect four rods with a diameter of 2–3mm (7/64–1/8in) to a tin can.

Use tissue paper to wrap around the frame.

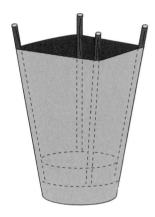

Use metal wire to connect the rods diagonally to each other.

Put a tea candle into the bottom of the container. Use tin foil to cover the upper part so that no air can enter.

Messenger kites

Messages can be carried up into the sky and pushed up the towline by the wind.

Cut out some circles with a diameter of 12–15cm (4³/₄–6in) from cardboard. Cut them along the radius and make a small hole in the centre.

Next, stick on a strip of crinkled paper. Run the towline through to the centre of the circle, which will quickly rise to the end of the kite with its long tail.

If you want your messages to be held at fixed points along the line, attach cardboard cones to it, but don't fix too many cones, or you will risk overloading the kite in terms of weight.

Here is a more complex design that involves a mechanism made of two rods made of bamboo or plastic, and a triangular sail that ensures that the message will be pulled up the towline.

The sail

Cut out an equilateral triangle – 40cm (1ft 4in) each side – from spinnaker nylon. Hem the fabric and insert three bamboo rods into the appropriate pocket fastenings.

The guide

Cut a section of bamboo about 7–8cm (2³/₄–3¹/₈in) with no nodes. Make two deep incisions halfway along it. Use very thin metal wire or adhesive tape to connect it to another section of bamboo. Then attach two rings for connecting the message to the towline.

Position the sail and connect one of the points of the triangle to the rod. Insert the metal wire into the bamboo cane. Make sure that at least 10cm (4in) comes out of the end, and use it to make a hook to connect to the line of the kite.

Bend the line that comes out of the opposite end and insert it into the lower cane. Now hook on the message to be released.

Once you have fastened the rings to the towline, the message will rise and then block against the obstacles that you have already placed along the line.

When the message is unhooked it will be released. The ring that held the small sail open will also be released. As the sail is no longer supported by the wind, it will return to you.

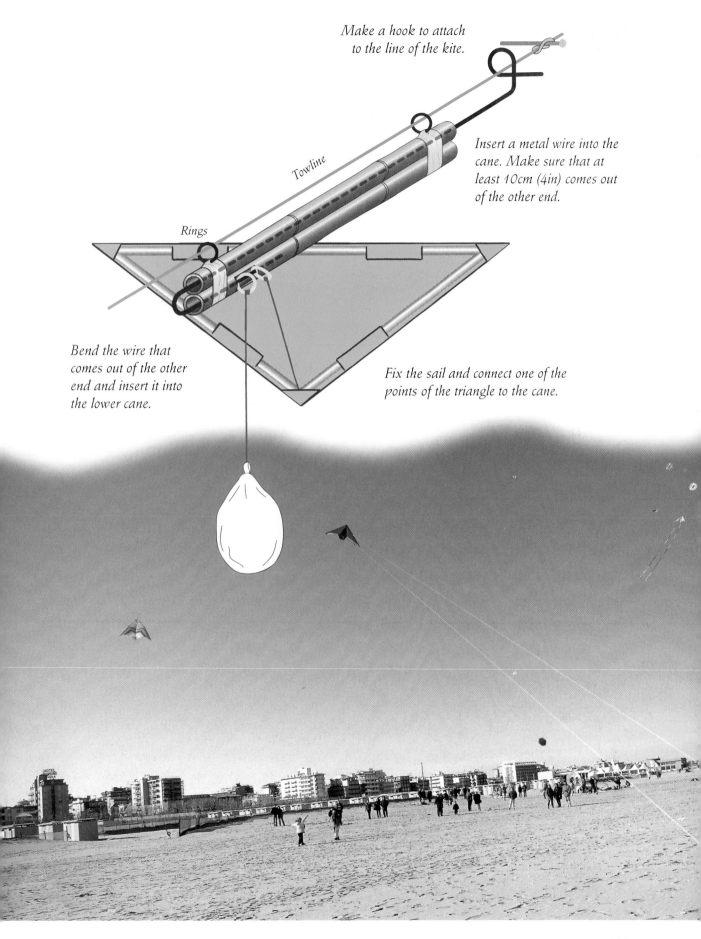

Make a hook to attach to the line of the kite.

Insert a metal wire into the cane. Make sure that at least 10cm (4in) comes out of the other end.

Towline

Rings

Bend the wire that comes out of the other end and insert it into the lower cane.

Fix the sail and connect one of the points of the triangle to the cane.

Parachutes

You can use a messenger kite to raise photographic equipment or a video camera, or just to send messages. You can also attach a parachute or gliders, which will unhook automatically when they meet the kite.

Take a piece of tissue paper and fold it, then fold it again. Next, fold it along the diagonal, starting from the centre of the sheet of paper, as shown.

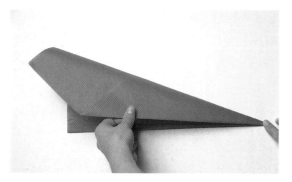

Fold the corner to the centre of the sheet. Repeat the procedure.

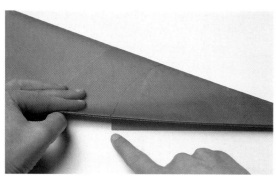

Cut the paper, starting from the point indicated in the illustration left by the position of the index finger of the right hand.

Do not waste your time when there is no wind. Your kite will not rise. Wait until the wind conditions are more favourable. In the meantime you can make windsocks or parachutes.

Open the sheet. It will look like a big flower.

Use adhesive tape to fix a line to the centre of the eight petals.

Fold the sheet of paper back on itself.

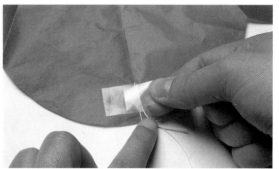

Take the metal piece from the centre of a clothes peg and connect the two flat parts together.

Use metal wire, paper and felt pens to provide shape and form to the little parachutist figure.

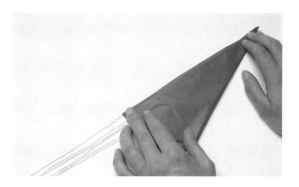

Attach it to the parachute.

Fold the parachute in such a way that you can hold it in the palm of your hand and throw it into the air with great force.

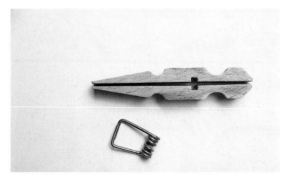

Once your parachute is in the air, it will open. Then it will begin to drop towards the ground slowly and gracefully.

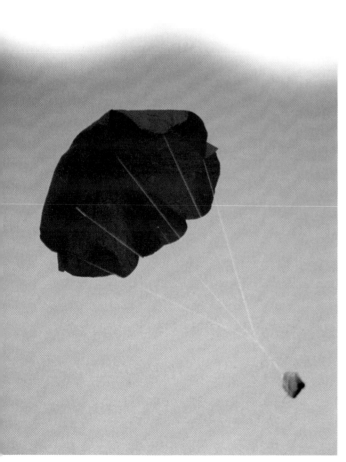

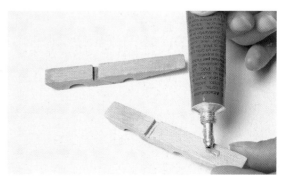

Materials and Equipment

Kite Construction

Kites in Flight